Table of Contents

MW01155406

THE COIN COLLECTING BIBLE 2023

6 IN 1

THE ULTIMATE GUIDE FOR BEGINNERS TO START YOUR COIN COLLECTION | HOW TO IDENTIFY, VALUE, PRESERVE AND GROW YOUR WEALTH

BY

John Adams

INTRODUCTION

Collecting coins or other manufactured legal currency is known as coin collecting. Rare coins, coins having mint flaws, and particularly lovely or historically important coins are frequently among the coins of fascination to collectors. Although the two fields are closely related, collecting coins can be distinguished from numismatics, which is the scientific study of money as a whole.

Coin albums are used by certain numismatists to store their vintage coins. A key factor in determining a coin's value is its grade. Most coins can be graded, authenticated, assigned attributes, and encapsulated by commercial groups.

You can adopt a hobby like a coin collecting at whatever age, and it can be around for a long time. Since you can examine the coins which you currently have and determine how they integrate into your collection, it's a relatively simple pastime to start. Additionally, this pastime is a fantastic method to spark an interest in subjects like math, archaeology, & history. There're numerous ways to amass coins. Saving coins that you find in circulation is the easiest method, and that's how several of the best collectors made their debut. For instance, some novices hunt for a coin of every date & mintmark variety in an effort to finish a group of Lincoln Cents that are still in circulation. A coin's mintmark, which might be a letter or symbol, identifies the mint from which it was minted. As new collectors learn some dates and mintmarks are more difficult to track down than others, they might look to such a coin dealer to purchase an instance to complete a gap in their collection.

The activity of coin collecting has been around since the 12th century & is still very popular today. There are several various motivations for beginning a coin collection, also referred to as "numismatics" among hobbyists. Collecting specific £1, £2, or 50p coins from spare change is among the cheapest methods to start collecting. They'll rarely lose value, & you can spend them if you get bored with the activity. For some owners, the delight comes from being able to completely comprehend an exquisite work of art's age, weight, as well as history while holding it in the center of their hand. Rare artifacts are typically prized for their brilliance and rarity & are occasionally sought after utilizing metal detectors.

Whatever your reason for being involved in numismatics, this overview of ancient coins will teach you some fundamental principles so you may build a collection you'll be pleased with.

BOOK 1.
THE BASICS OF COLLECTING

Chapter 1.
Why Coin Collecting?

Welcome to the world of coin collecting!

Several historians agree that coin collecting first started in Asia. People started to use coins as a way of exchange for goods and services by the time the Middle Ages began. It's not a secret that the first Chinese coins were made out of bronze while Roman coins were minted out of silver. The first coins minted in Europe were gold and silver double-struck pieces called bezants that were minted in the year 772 in Constantinople, which is now known as Istanbul, Turkey. These coins were used as an accepted form of currency until Gutenberg printed his own version of the book called "The Gutenberg Bible" which means that people would trade different versions for one or they used to buy their books with them as well. These coins were more easily accepted because the face on them was similar to the current coins that people used. The Byzantine Empire's currency was called "Tetraevangelia" which means "the four gospels". For this reason, it was thought that pieces of the face of Christ should be on them so it became a tradition for people to put his image on their coins. Around the year 919, Charlemagne minted an extremely valuable coin called a "solidus" which represented the gold content in an ounce and had a portrait of him on it saying "Patefim Sacrum."

Today, there are three basic types of coins: Minted coins, private-issue (such as state and municipal), and commemorative. Coins are made from five metals: copper, nickel, zinc, silver, and gold. The most usual type of coin is the silver coin minted by the US government which is called the American Eagle. Probably, this is also the coin that you are more familiar with. However, not all coins are minted in the US because some countries do not have a government in place to mint their own money. An example of this would be Canada, which issues their own coins with the face of Queen Elizabeth II on them or Australia, which issues them with a kangaroo. Another example that you were probably not aware of is Kuwait. Coins in Kuwait have pictures of the king along with several other symbols including camels. However, I really can't avoid telling you why coin collecting is also often referred to as "the hobby of the kings". The reason for this is that during The Renaissance time in the largest European countries such as France and Germany having a coin collection was extremely expensive and only wealthy and powerful families could afford to own a private coin collection. Today, you are lucky because you don't need to be a king (even if you feel you are) to start your own coin collection.

Today, coin collectors enjoy collecting, trading, and exchanging coins for many different reasons. Some people collect coins because it is a fun hobby, others do it for investment purposes and some even combine both of those reasons to collect coins. Some do it accidentally because they get fascinated by coins especially, from many generations back. Others take it very seriously and keep coins in order to preserve history. However, every coin collector I spoke with during my life always struggles when they decide to sell their coins. This is the reason why one thing many coin collectors do with their old or expired coins is to donate them to charity or to family members as gifts.

Summing up, everyone starts to collect coins for their own reasons. Your reason is different from any other coin collector.

Personally, I love to collect coins because I love history, and being the owner of a coin makes me feel part of that frame. It's like traveling back in time without a time machine. Doesn't it feel great to have a coin that existed in the 1700s when you were not in existence? I don't know you, but I would feel like I was going back in time and experiencing the times of Abraham Lincoln.

Before starting with the nitty-gritty of coin collecting, let's have a more detailed look at the most common reasons why people do start coin collecting. I hope that before starting your coin collection you have already decided your reason to start.

Which category do you fall in?

Collecting as an Investment

Some collectors are after coins for their monetary value. These collectors look for high-quality, rare and in-demand coins that can fetch high prices among numismatic connoisseurs. This is because there are coins made of valuable metals such as silver and gold; others are rare and may be sold for millions of dollars. The current most valuable coin is the 1907 Saint-Gaudens Double Eagle which is worth $7 million US. Yes, you read right: $7 million US.

If it's your primary goal to sell off your coins you will need to do a lot of research about coins to learn their value, the materials particular coins are made of, and keep up with market trends to know which ones are on demand. This will enable you to make smart acquisition decisions so that you can have a great investment.

It is important to understand that you may not get a return on your investment immediately or within the next ten years. If you are in this, brace yourself to be in it for the long haul. If you are making smart decisions on your acquisitions now, you will have great returns in the future.

John J Pittman Jr., the famous coin collector and numismatist, assembled a world-class coin collection over many decades. He searched for exceptional coins, high in value and rare that he could afford, and added them to his collection. In 1997, David W. Akers sold this exceptional coin collection for 30 million dollars! In this collection was a proof 1883

Capped Head gold five-dollar half eagle coin, which he bought for $635 in 1954. In 1997, it had increased in value and sold for $467,500! Imagine that. So much profit was made and all because of one valuable thing that John applied when collecting coins as an investment, which is Knowledge. You have got to know your coins.

If you decide to start coin collecting as an investment you should really become an expert and become able to spot the value of a coin. In the past, coin collectors have given up their possession of coins due to the fact that they could no longer afford them or because inflation caused a drastic change in their values. It is for these reasons that several people give up on their hobby and turn to other things they enjoy now. It is not uncommon for someone to collect coins and then lose interest before realizing that there was a huge increase in value from what they had originally collected. Inflation can cause serious problems for coin collectors as well as people who own stocks or bonds.

Coin collecting is similar to every other investment. They depreciate in worth, and other coins may experience an uphill climb. The ideal method to profit from coin collecting is to be up-to-date with the news and the routine coin prices. This will assist you not to be deceived by numerous merchants but to help in finding out how to price a coin even without a catalog.

Collecting coins for investment can also be dangerous because some coins are highly demanded and fake copies are made, some counterfeiters have been caught by the government before and have been held accountable for the distribution of such counterfeit coins.

To Learn About History

Some people collect coins to document history. Imagine holding in your hands a 1943 US penny made of zinc-coated steel other than the usual copper they use nowadays, or an ancient coin with a portrait of earlier century leaders such as Alexander the Great. It's cool to have pieces of history with you. It's evidence of the existence of generations before us and shows us just how far we have come. It takes you back in time when you were not in existence. It is fascinating to be a historical coin collector.

These people collect coins by date, mint mark, country of origin, condition (scratched or not) and a variety of other factors. They love to categorize them into collections like commemorative coins for any specific event such as the Olympic Games or Winston Churchill's birthdays with their family crest on it or specific medals and tokens for sports championships.

Here the focus is mostly on the calendar, which year the coin was made, any special event that was marked during that time, whose portrait is on it, and so on. Research it for the history behind each coin, which you can document and label on the coin case or wherever you choose to put them (We shall discuss more on proper coin storage).

As a Hobby; for Fun!

Some are in it for the thrill of assembling a collection. They may be excited to track down a rare coin, to finish a particular set of coins or they may be appreciating the artistic value of the coins.

If you are doing it for fun, it does not matter what coins you collect if they are orderly arranged in your collection. Throwing coins in a piggy bank is not making a collection. You need to arrange and classify your coins in a way that you can identify them and connect them with the reason they ended up in your collection. For instance, you can have a category for rare coins from the 18th century, new coins for the 20th century; the now 'extinct' zinc-coated steel coins, and so on. Other than that, collect whatever gives you that 'thrill'.

To Pass on to Future Generations

A coin collection could be one of the most valuable things you pass on to your kids. It could be your legacy, to live on even after you are gone. You see, if we could face reality, it looks like paper or coin money may not exist in the coming generations. People are already adopting crypto currency and other forms of intangible currency. Who knows, it may be what people use to transact business in the coming days.

How precious will tangible money in form of a coin collection then be? It will be a precious gift to own. Also, as coins increase in value over time, and their rarity in the coming days considered, your collection will be a gold mine. The coming generations may benefit greatly from your decision to start this hobby. Finding and owning those coins is going to bring you so much joy. You see, every coin that you manage to add to your collection is an achievement. It's exciting as well as fulfilling!

Chapter 2.
Different Kinds of Coins

Now it is actually the time for you to dive deeper and learn about the different kinds of coins (as well as their specificities).

Coins can be categorized according to different criteria (such as the material used for making them, for example, or the event on which they were created). However, to make it all simpler for you, we will not go too in-depth into the exact categories, but present you the main types of coins in general.

Gold and Silver Coins

Ever since ancient times, most countries have used gold and silver coins as their currency. This includes Ancient Rome, Ancient Greece, Egypt, and even England and the United States.

Gold and silver coins are not used anymore in everyday transactions, but they are definitely among the most wanted pieces for collectors. Depending on what gold or silver coin you might be looking for, the price for such a piece can get quite steep.

Commemorative Coins

Commemorative coins in the United States started to be popular in the 1930s when law required the US Mint to strike them. They were sold to distributors who also added a premium on top of the actual value of the coin. However, this did not last for a long period of time, as collectors started to complain about speculators manipulating the prices and the market. As such, the US Mint started to produce fewer commemorative coins.

The first wave of commemorative coins attracted a lot of people into coin collecting, just as they are today as well. To the date, commemorative coins are considered to be appealing and beautiful not only for collectors, but even for people who don't have much to do with coin collecting in general.

Revolutionary Coins

In short, revolutionary coins are coins that circulated in times of revolution (such as the American Revolution of 1776, for example). Because of the historical significance they bear, these coins can be quite valuable (but this depends on other factors too).

Ancient Coins

Ancient coins are sometimes considered synonymous to gold or silver coins. However, this actually might not always be the case, as other materials were used in ancient times for the manufacturing of coins as well (such as glass, ivory, or porcelain, for example).

Furthermore, another misconception many people have about ancient coins is that they are extremely expensive. This might be the case in some situations, but you can still own one (or more) without breaking the bank, as the market value of a coin is not determined by its age only.

Souvenir Pennies

These coins are quite interesting. Basically, they are normal coins that have been pressed, elongated, and redesigned. The most interesting fact about them actually, is that mutilating coins with the purpose of putting them back into circulation again is illegal, with the exception of these souvenir pennies. Definitely a quirky addition to any collector's files!

Medallions

The word "medallion" is frequently used to describe a variety of types of coins (including commemorative coins). As a general rule, "medallions" are pretty much any type of round, decorated piece of metal that has some sort of significance attached to it (such as monetary value, for example). However, most often, actual medallions do not have a legal tender attached to them.

Tokens

Trade tokens tend to be quite rare and very collectible. Most often, these tokens were created in times of financial trouble when silver and gold were scarce, and yet people still needed something for their currency.

Tokens were usually valued at $1 or less at their face value, but there are tokens that can go as high as $5, for example. Just like "normal" circulated coins, they were used in everyday transactions.

Error Coins

Basically, these coins were manufactured with an error (such as a double denomination, overdate, or brokerage). They came out of the mint this way, and some might be tempted to believe they are not valuable at all. However, depending on the defect and depending on the era they came from, error coins can be quite pricey as well.

BU Rolls

BU Rolls are very representative for the new wave of coin collecting enthusiasts at the end of the actual 1950s and the beginning of the 1960s. These "rolls" were bank-wrapped Brilliant Uncirculated small stashes of coins that made collectors go crazy in the era. Their

15-minute of fame started to fade out when collectors realized that, although some of these BU rolls were advertised as rare, they were, in fact, quite the opposite (as they had been manufactured by the millions). As such, BU Rolls tend to be shockingly cheap these days, so you might want to avoid falling into a trap on them.

Silver Certificates

Old Silver Certificates were used by people to redeem one silver dollar. However, these certificates were only valid up to 1964 when the government discontinued their manufacturing. For a while though, people were allowed to redeem their silver certificates for a given amount of silver - which eventually turned into a whole new craze in the coin collecting world as everyone was "suddenly" looking for these.

Clearly, just like other fads, this trend attracted a lot of people towards the coin collecting world.

Art Bars

Somewhat an oddity, art bars were very popular in the 1970s. They were thin, rectangular silver bars weighing one ounce and they had polished surfaces and designs meant to commemorate pretty much everything you can imagine: from your wedding to your cat.

At first, mintages were limited, so art bars were very sought after. Like the other types of coins presented in our list which led to a new trend, art bars attracted a lot of collectors to the world of coins as well.

There's no actual right or wrong type of coin to collect. Sure, some have more value today while others don't, but at the end of the day the value does not always only lie in the type of coin, as much as it lies in a variety of factors.

Chapter 3.
Numimastic Language

Coin collectors speak a unique language and use specific terms when discussing coin collecting like any other community or social group. Do you want to spend time with other numismatists and have no idea what they say when talking about this fascinating subject? To make matters worse, approaching a coin dealer and insisting on explaining every term isn't a pleasant experience. If you don't speak the language, you're at risk of being taken advantage of because it's easy to be fooled if you don't know your way around coins.

Numismatics is generally defined as the systematic acquisition and study of coins. As a result, coin collecting has become a subset of numismatics. Numismatics encompasses a wide range of money-related items, including coins, tokens, currency, checks, medals, stock certificates, and other items that represent current and past financial assets or liabilities. Numismatists include those who study the field of numismatics and coin collectors.

Although no one will actually ever tell you this, picking up the lingo is the best way to blend in and get the hang of any new practice. "Language even more than color defines who you are to people," wrote Trevor Noah in his book 'Born a crime' He was able to get by with the help of language during a time when people of his skin tone were subjected to racial profiling. The ability to speak the language of a specific social group gives you a significant advantage in the workplace. You'll be able to converse with dealers, fellow numismatists, and other coin collectors more easily. Numismatic terms and their definitions are listed below.

Terms Related to the Condition of a Coin

About Good (A.G.): It's not great, but it's also not terrible to say that a coin is "about good" because the grade of the coins is just below good. Only the most important characteristics are likely to be discernible on an A.G. coin.

Features like the mintmark, the date, and so forth are included. Some other features like portraits may also have faded away.

Abrasions: If someone says, "This coin has abrasions," or in other words, the coin has been abraded by another coin, a foreign object, or some substance (like acid).

Alternate surfaces: A coin with an altered surface is referred to, that its value has been diminished due to factors such as cleaning or polishing, making it unattractive to collectors.

Uncirculated: A coin is considered "uncirculated" if it hasn't been used in a day-to-day transaction.

Almost uncirculated: This coin appears to be brand new to the naked eye or at first glance as if it has never been circulated. A magnifying glass can reveal minor friction or rubs if examined closely.

No Grade: A coin that returns from a third-party grading service and is not encapsulated is referred to as having "no grade." Authenticity or damage could be to blame.

Artificial Toning: To add color by using chemicals or heat on the coin's surface is a form of artificial toning.

Bag Toning: A coin can acquire some color when stored in a cloth bag containing sulfur and other metal-reactive chemicals, such as those found in sulphuric acid. Morgan silver dollars tend to develop bag toning.

Brown: The term "brown" refers to a copper coin that has lost its red color due to various factors. The word "brown" can be abbreviated as B.N. when describing a coin in grading.

Alteration refers to a coin with its mintmark or date altered to make it appear to be a rare or valuable issue.

A Carbon Spot: Discoloration on the surface of a coin is known as a "carbon spot." A planchet imperfection before the coin's striking and improper storage is possible causes. Carbon spots are nearly impossible to remove without leaving pits on the surface, no matter the reason. Carbon spots diminish the value and quality of a coin.

Basal State: A coin is said to be in this state if it's in a condition consistent with its basic form, which means that it can only be identified by the mintmark, date, and type of the coin. One-year coins may not have a visible date on them.

A Cleaned Coin: It will likely lose its natural color and luster and appear washed out if treated with baking soda. A coin that has been "cleaned" is referred to as such.

Questionable Toning: The term refers to the suspicion that a coin's color is artificial, not natural.

Raw: Ungraded coins are known as "raw" in this context.

Semi-Commons: Coins classified as semi-common fall in the middle of the rarity and commonness spectrum.

Ultra-Rare: Coins or numismatic artifacts that are extremely rare are included in this category. Only a few examples/pieces of evidence are needed.

Terms Used to Describe Characteristics

Bust: In a coin's bust design, the head, neck, and upper shoulders are all included.

Denomination: The face value of each coin is referred to as "denomination." When you inquire about a coin's "denomination," you're referring to its actual weight.

Face values: A coin's "face value" refers to its legal issue. One pound, one dollar, or fifty pence is the unit of measure.

Coin attributes: the parts of a coin that make up its design, grade, luster, strike, and marks; these are the primary characteristics and the ability to catch the eye.

Mintmark: Coins are identified by the mintmark, a small letter that appears on the coin's surface or the place where it was struck, the mint.

Relief: An area of a coin's design, known as a relief, is raised above the rest of the coin's surface.

The Incuse: This refers to the coin's legal issue. So, for example, is one dollar, one pound, or 50 pence.

Legal Tender: a form of money recognized by the government: A type of currency issued and exchanged for financial transactions.

Bi-metallic: This coin is bi-metallic, which means it is made of two different metals at once.

Circulation: It means how much a coin has worth in the real world. Coins that have been used in transactions are also referred to as "spent coins."

Arrows: On most U.S. coins, you'll see this design element in the left claw of the eagle.

Observe: Known as "heads," a front side of a coin

Reverse: Known as "tails," a backside of a coin.

Terms related to Mint Place:

C: This mint mark identifies where a coin was struck at the Charlotte, NC mint.

S-mint: San Francisco mint coins are referred to as S-minted coins.

Classic Era: Coins from the classic era were produced between 1792 and 1964, during which time silver and gold coins were in circulation of the United States were made available for public use; they were meant to be spent in commerce. The 'classic era' refers to this time.

Lister: When discussing coins, the term "luster" refers to the coin's ability to reflect light. It's a tool for grading coins. However, luster should be used with caution when grading a coin because it can be difficult to tell if it is artificial or natural, depending on how it was made. The luster of a surface can be reduced by cleaning, wear, and friction.

Terms of Denominations

Penny: Another name for a one-cent coin in the United States is a "penny."

Nickel: Five-cent U.S. coins are commonly referred to as nickels.

Dime: A dime is one-tenth of a U.S. dollar (10 cents).

Some Other Terms:

Pedigree: The most valuable coins, such as rare bullion coins, have a higher pedigree. A coin's pedigree is a list of the current owner's information and every one of its predecessors.

Set: When you have a collection of something, you can say you have a set from a specific batch of coins. As an illustration, think of an actual group of half-dollars from a particular mint.

Chapter 4.
What coins are worth buying?

Depending on the kind of coin collector you are, you might want to look after one or more of the following coin characteristics when considering whether or not to buy them:

- **Denomination:** Every currency puts out different denominations (such as the penny, the nickel, the dime, and the quarter, for example). If you want to go big, you could start collecting denominations that are obsolete as well (such as the 20-cent coin, for example).

- **Type:** This does not necessarily refer to the type of coins, but to the designs available for each denomination. For instance, a half dollar could be a Flowing Hair, a Franklin head, a Seated Liberty, a Walking Liberty, and so on.

- **Date:** Some people collect coins by the date they were issued, and that is perfectly fine. For instance, you might want to collect all types of nickels that were issued from 1900 to the current date (and you can also choose to skip the very rare and expensive ones if that is what you want).

- **Date and mintmark combination:** You might also want to collect coins according to the date and mintmark. Do keep in mind that this can be more expensive than just collecting them according to their date because most coin series have a particular mintmark that is very pricey. This is not true for all types of coins (in the sense described in the second bullet point in this list). For instance, collecting all the Barber dimes might get prohibitively expensive (as the rare ones can cost as much as $1,000,000). However, collecting all the Barber half-dollar coins might be affordable.

- **Year:** This type of collection includes all the coins issued in the year of your birth. If you are under 50 years old, doing this will be quite easy as you can just buy Mint sets. However, you might also want to set a different challenge (such as collecting all coins released in another year of significance for you or for history in general).

Now, I realize all this could be a little confusing when you are just starting out your coin collection, but don't worry: as long as you are curious and read as much as you can on the topic, you will definitely get all the ins and outs of this lucrative hobby.

BOOK 2.
DETERMINING THE VALUE OF A COIN

Chapter 1.
How to Determine the Value of a Coin

Looking back into history, you'd find out that the value of coins are generally corresponded to their actual metallic composition. But now, circulating coins have been said to amount to some value merely because the government says so. This is called fiat money.

The following are some factors that make a coin valuable:

Mintage

The number one factor that is used in determining the actual value of a particular coin (down to the actual date and mintmark) is its mintage. A mintage number is used to indicate the number of examples of that given issue that was produced at first in the United States Mint. When the mintage is low, it signifies that the number of coins available is less than the interested collectors.

However, Mintage is not the only factor that affects the value of a coin in terms of quality. Of course, Mintage is important. It shows the number of specimens that may exist in the actual largest possible pool of a certain coin. But a lot of collectors fixate just on the mintage numbers when they should also look out for the coin's population estimate.

Demand

A few dozen of a particular kind of coin sounds quite limited, doesn't it? But would that be the case if only, say, five or ten people want one of those coins with 20 or 30 of them remaining?

In the case of the 1927-D Saint-Gaudens double eagle, there is a large number of collectors who want one of the coins and are also in a good financial position to plunk half a million dollars on the coin. On the other hand, several obscure foreign coins are quite limited in number. But, because people don't make collections on them, they can be had for a song.

So, why would you call a coin numbered up to tens of thousands rare? You would have to take a closer look. It all has to actually do with supply and demand.

Condition

Regardless of the kind of coin in question, the condition or state of the coin will always be a huge factor that affects the value of a coin. Condition isn't just a coin's wear-based grade. It also refers to the color or tone of the coin, signs of damage, and overall appearance.

Condition is said to be a very important factor because of the same reasons as mintage and population. After a few years, the coins that are kept safely tend to get scarcer. This relative scarcity, coupled with the demand of the collector shoots the prices straight up.

The best sources for checking the condition of a coin are third-party grading services like NGC and PCGS.

Age

Even though this isn't true in all cases, the older coins have more value. It is not just about the age but all the things that come with age:

- Older coins are usually scarcer as the coins tend to get missing or destroyed over time.

- The older a coin gets, the higher its chance of being worn out or damaged. With this, the number of that particular kind of coin diminishes.
- The availability of older coins tends to be lower. They can't be gotten straight from a mint and they might not even be in circulation.

So it is not certain that every old coin is better or worth more than a new coin. The age of a coin, coupled with everything related to its age, is simply an important factor to actually consider when determining the value of a coin. At times, coin collectors may put their focus on coins minted on precise dates. Depending on the year of a coin's mintage, it might be worth more than normal for collectible purposes.

Design

The design imprinted on a particular coin sends across different kinds of cultural, historical, and patriotic themes.

This attractive feature of coins has been quite frequent to all peoples in recorded world history. Even the coins from the old representations on coins pass information about a moment in history. Regardless of whether the coin had an emperor or indigenous fauna in it, it displays cultural values.

Here's how it affects the value of a coin:

A lot of people will like to pay extra amounts for a coin with a very attractive design. Collectors also find interest in designs. They can decide to make collections based on different designs imprinted on coins.

Bullion Content

Bullion content is referred to as the metallic composition of a coin. In layman's terms, it is the material used to make the coin.

The important question is how to determine the metal used to make a coin. It is not enough to assume just by looking at the colors. Most coins are usually only covered with gold and silver. You could even mistake a brass coin for a gold coin at first glance.

With the modern bullion coins, it is quite easy to tell. They are usually tagged with their precise weight and purity. Sometimes, you might have to carry out some extra testing to determine the metallic composition of a coin.

Burn Value

The precious metal's inherent worth in a coin, such as gold or silver, can significantly determine its value and price. Beginning in 1965, the United States started replacing the 90% silver content of its dimes, nickels, and half dollars with a base metal made of copper and nickel. Therefore, the prices and values of gold and silver coins may change by the price of gold and silver.

This is not merely applicable to precious metals. Copper and nickel prices have started to increase recently. People will actually start melting these common coins to benefit from the sale of the copper and nickel recovered from them if the value of the base metal in our present coinage surpasses the face value of the coin.

Retail Stock

The quantity of inventory a specific dealer has on hand can impact a coin's value and pricing. For instance, a dealer will be more inclined to lower the price if he has a large quantity of 1931-S uncirculated Lincoln cents in his inventory to sell more of them to collectors and lower his inventory. Conversely, if you try to sell the same dealer a 1931-S uncirculated Lincoln cent, he would probably offer you a lower price than you would anticipate because he already has more in stock. The opposite is accurate if he has a small number of coins in stock. Get many quotations from other coin dealers before you sell your coins.

Finally, a certain coin's entire supply on the market may alter significantly. A coin will lose value, for instance, if a coin hoard is discovered and sold all at once, regardless of the dealer's inventory. The price and the actual value of these coins would plummet significantly, for instance, if a case of 10,000 1931-S uncirculated Lincoln cents were discovered and the owner started to actually sell them all at once. Realizing many items are available for purchase, customers would choose the vendor offering the lowest price. As a result, dealers would start to reduce their prices to get rid of their inventory of these coins before the price fell much more.

Chapter 2.
Coin grading

The point grading scale is a system used to evaluate the condition of a coin and assign it a numerical grade based on a range of criteria. This scale can be used to determine the value of a coin and is often used by collectors and dealers to determine the worth of a coin.

The point grading scale typically ranges from 1 to 70, with the higher numbers indicating a coin that is in better condition. The grades are typically broken down into several categories:

1-49: Poor to Fair

50-53: About Good

54-57: Good

58-61: Very Good

62-65: Fine

66-69: Very Fine

70: Uncirculated (also known as Mint State)

To determine a coin's grade, a number of factors are taken into account, including the coin's overall appearance, the amount of wear on the coin, the level of detail present, and the presence of any defects. The exact criteria and definitions for each grade can vary slightly depending on the coin and the grading system being used. The order of preservation refers to the condition of a coin and how well it has been preserved over time. Coins that have been well-preserved will generally be in better condition than those that have not been as well-preserved.

There are several factors that can impact the order of preservation of a coin, including the type of metal the coin is made of, how it was stored, and the environment it has been exposed to. For example, a coin made of gold or silver will generally be more resistant to wear and deterioration than a coin made of a less durable metal, and a coin that has been stored in a cool, dry place will generally be in better condition than one that has been stored in a damp or humid environment.

The Order of preservation (also known as the point grading scale) is a system used to evaluate the condition of a coin and assign it a numerical grade based on a range of criteria. The grades on the scale range from 1 to 70, with higher numbers indicating a coin that is in better condition.

Here is a brief overview of the grades on the point grading scale:

- Basal State (PO): This is the lowest grade on the scale and indicates a coin that is in extremely poor condition, with little or no detail remaining.
- Fair (Fr): A coin in Fair condition will show significant wear and may be heavily circulated. It will have some detail remaining, but it will be difficult to make out.
- About or Almost Good (AG): A coin in About Good condition will show heavy wear and may be well-circulated. It will have some detail remaining, but it will be faint.
- Good (G): A coin in Good condition will show moderate to heavy wear and may have been heavily circulated. It will have some detail remaining, but it will be faint.
- Very Good (VG): A coin in Very Good condition will show moderate wear and may have been circulated. It will have most of its detail remaining, but it may be worn or faded.
- Fine (F): A coin in Fine condition will show light to moderate wear and may have been circulated. It will have most of its detail remaining, but it may be worn or faded.
- Very Fine (VF): A coin in Very Fine condition will show light wear and may have been circulated. It will have most of its detail remaining and may have some minor imperfections.
- Extremely Fine (EF): A coin in Extremely Fine condition will show minimal wear and may have been circulated. It will have all of its detail remaining and may have some minor imperfections.

- Almost or About Uncirculated (AU): A coin in About Uncirculated condition will show almost no wear and may have been lightly circulated. It will have all of its detail remaining and may have some minor imperfections.
- Uncirculated (Unc): A coin in Uncirculated condition, also known as Mint State, will show no wear and will not have been circulated. It will have all of its detail remaining and may have some minor imperfections.
- Brilliant Uncirculated (BU): A coin in Brilliant Uncirculated condition will be in the same condition as a coin in Uncirculated condition, but it will have a particularly high level of luster and eye appeal.

Chapter 3.
A Guide to Coin Values

Below, I have included a basic guide to the prices and year of some of the best-known and most valuable coins.

5 Cents Buffalo Nickel (1913 - 1938), $7.900 - $15.200

Peace Dollars (1923), $30.80 - $39.70. Uncirculated condition sell up to $3.790

Indian Head Eagles (1907 – 1933), $610.00 - $760.00

Indian Half Eagles (1908 – 1929), $320.00 - $510.00

Bust Dollars Draped Bust, Small Eagle Reverse (1795 – 1798), $530.00 - $1,520.00

Early Dollars Flowing Hair (1794 – 1795), $510.00 - $2,540.00

Gold Dollars Liberty Head w/stars on front (1849 – 1854), $135.00 - $220.00

Half Cents Liberty Cap, Head Facing Right (1794 - 1797), $140.00 - $1,560.00

Bust Half Dimes Draped Bust, Heraldic Eagle Reverse (1800 - 1805), $160.00 - $1,230.00

Early Half Dollars Flowing Hair (1794 - 1795), $260.00 - $2,200.00

Early Eagles Capped Bust Right, Small Eagle (1795 - 1797), $5.200.00 - $15.100.00

Liberty Eagles Coronet (1838 – 1907), $630.00 - $740.00

Early Eagles Capped Bust Right, Heraldic Eagle (1797 - 1804), $1,780.00 - $5,200.00

Classic Quarter Eagles (1834 - 1839), $235.00 - $530.00

Facing Left (1808), $7,400.00 - $20,200.00

Three Dollar Gold Pieces (1854 - 1889), $510.00 - $2,300.00

Early Half Eagles Capped Bust Left (1807 - 1812), $1.100.00 - $2.600.00

Early Half Eagles Capped Bust Right, Small Eagle (1795 - 1798), $4,300.00 - $10,200.00

Liberty Quarter Eagles Coronet (1840 - 1907), $210.00 - $360.00

Liberty Head V Nickel (1913), $4,230,955

Edward III Florin (I343), $6,900,000

Brasher Doubloon (I787), $9,990,500

Saint-Gaudens (1933), $20,175,100

Saint-Gaudens Double Eagle (1907), $2200 - $2085

St Gaudens Double Eagle (1931), $22100.00 - $125,000.00

S Liberty Seated Dollar (1870), $175000.00 - $1,960,995.00

O Capped Bust Half Dollar (1838), $160000.00 - $750,000.00

Draped Bust Half Dollar (1797), $20000.00 - $510,000.00

Steel Wheat Penny (1944), $10000.00 - $410,000.00

D Walking Liberty Half Dollar (1919), $30.00 - $180,600.00

CC Liberty Seated Dollar (1871), $3360.00 - $172,000.00

CC Liberty Seated Dollar (1873), $9000.00 - $165,098.00

Umayyad Gold Dinar (723AD), $5,407,400

S Barber Dime (1894), $2,409,200

Lincoln Head Copper Penny (1943), $2,340,200

Sacagawea Cheerios Dollar (2000), $26,000

BOOK 3.
DETECTING FAKE OR COUNTERFEIT COINS

Chapter 1.
Where to Buy Coins

Keep in mind that counterfeit coins can still be a problem at coin shops – many owners deal in a high amount of volume, so they may not always have time to thoroughly authenticate each coin before putting it out for sale.

"Caveat emptor" applies here – coin shops do not often label coins as having been cleaned or damaged. Take a close look at any coin before buying it, preferably with some sort of magnification.

Online Coin Dealers

With the rise of the internet and of eCommerce, more and more coin dealers are selling their coins online. Large national dealers like APMEX and Littleton offer wide selections, though not usually at prices as competitive as eBay.

Individual coin dealers like myself specialize in specific niches, often with deeper catalogs for those niches than could otherwise be found on eBay.

Find a seller you like on eBay? Do a quick Google search on their username to see if they have a separate website. Many of the larger sellers do, and you'll find the same coins they have on eBay for cheaper prices on their website thanks to the lack of selling fees.

Coin Auction Houses

As you progress in the hobby, you may find your interests evolving to higher-value coins. Auction houses like Heritage Auctions, GreatCollections, and Stack's Bowers offer rarer and more valuable coins than what you'll find on eBay. Keep in mind that the bidding competition is usually fierce, and these coins go for premium prices. Also worth noting is that many of these auction houses (unlike eBay) have a "buyer's premium" fee of an additional 15-20% on top of the final auction price.

There are many places where you can purchase coins. Some common options include:

Coin stores: These are specialty stores that sell coins and often other numismatic items as well. You can find coin stores in many cities, or you can shop online through a coin store's website.

Coin shows: Coin shows are events where coin dealers and collectors come together to buy, sell, and trade coins. You can often find a wide variety of coins at a coin show, and it's a great way to meet other collectors and learn more about the hobby.

International fairs: These events, which are held in many countries around the world, offer an opportunity to purchase coins from different parts of the globe.

Other coin collectors: You may be able to find coins for sale through online marketplaces or through local coin collecting groups. You may also be able to purchase coins from individual collectors who are looking to sell part of their collection.

No matter where you decide to purchase coins, it's important to do your research and be an informed buyer. Make sure you understand the value and rarity of the coins you're considering, and be cautious of anyone who is trying to sell you a coin at an excessively high price.

Best Practices for Buying Coins

Buy what you know

Too many new collectors are lured in by a "great deal" on coins they know little about. Unfortunately, great deals in the coin collecting world are few and far between – most sellers know what they have, and price it accordingly.

This goes back to #1 of our 5 Principles of Coin Collecting, "Buy the book before you buy the coin." Knowledge is power, and it will benefit you immensely to have at least a basic knowledge of market prices, rarity, and grading techniques before purchasing a coin.

I understand that this can sometimes be difficult to commit to, and I admit that I don't always practice what I preach. Sometimes I might come across a neat-looking coin that I just have to have, even though I know next to nothing about it.

When that happens, I'll try to quickly do a search on eBay to see what comparable coins are selling for, or have sold for in the past. And I'll also restrict myself to cheaper coins – I'm not going to drop $500 on a coin I know nothing about. It may also be worthwhile to ask the dealer to reserve the coin for you – many are willing to do this, which will help give you a couple extra days to conduct some research.

Study the coin carefully

This may sound like common sense, but be sure to take the time to study the coin on both sides.

If buying online, that means looking at each of the photos and carefully examining the surfaces. If the photos are out of focus or uncropped, contact the seller to ask for better pictures. Keep in mind that the seller may purposefully be trying to conceal something with bad photos.

When viewing online photos, zoom in as much as possible to determine if the seller has edited the photos – common photo-doctoring techniques include the following:

- Editing out a mark or scratch by copying another part of the coin's surface and pasting it over the mark.
- Increasing the color saturation to make the coin's colors appear more vivid – this is an especially big problem with toned coins. This can usually be detected by looking at the color of other areas of the photo like the background and seeing if they appear normal or unnaturally vibrant.
- Not properly white balancing the camera before taking a photo (usually unintentional), causing the coin's colors to appear off. As with saturation, look at other areas of the photo to determine if the colors are natural. Silver coins should generally look grey or silver in color, and gold coins yellow/orange or gold.
- Taking a zoomed out or uncropped photo, making the coin itself very small and hard to see.

If you identify any of the above, reconsider whether you really want to buy the coin – the seller may either be concealing something or trying to make the coin look nicer than it actually is.

If buying in person, pick the coin or coin holder up by the edges and rotate it to catch the light. This will help reveal any light scratches or marks that might otherwise go undetected, and will also reveal any remaining mint luster on the coin.

Use a jeweler's loupe or small magnifying glass to get a closer look at the surfaces. I generally recommend a 5 or 10x magnification jeweler's loupe, which should cost you about $10 on Amazon or at your local coin shop. Using a loupe is permitted behavior at a coin shop or coin show, and any coin dealer unwilling to let you take that close of a look may be hiding something.

Chapter 2.
Finding Fake Coins

How to Discover Fake Coins

A special device does the coin stamping to make them real. Individuals who counterfeit coins are well trained and have the capability to manipulate those uncommon coins, which have high worth amongst collectors. The most typical process in counterfeiting is putting fluid metal into molds which are going to leave die marks with breaking on the fake coin.

Those who are professionals in identifying fake coins have actually observed that the modifications seen in the coins have actually added, eliminated, and even changed the coin's date markings. If an individual believes that he remains in the ownership of a fake collectible coin, he can attempt to get his other collections, that are supposed to be authentic and have the identical worth. He could then contrast the two coins to see wheter there are any markings on the fake one.

If the coin's worth is actually more than 5 cents, search for corrugations in the external the coin edges. These are really thin railings on the the coins edges. They additionally call this "reeding." Authentic coins have extremely thin edges, and they are uniformly distinct if one is really watchful. Those coins which are fake could be differentiated if the edges are not sufficiently thin.

Should there be circumstances in which an individual has actually received a fake coin, he must not return the fake coin to the individual that sent it to him. He needs to attempt to delay the individual in any circumstance. If the individual runs, he needs to attempt to keep him in sight. He ought to remember the individual's clothing and physical look and attempt to remember if the individual has any buddy throughout the exchange. If they have a vehicle, get the vehicle's plate number and call the nearby authorities for assistance right away.

There are numerous things which could be taken into consideration when recognizing whether the coin is fake or not:

1. A coin restrike could be used to recognize verified coins. These coins are really dated earlier than those initially released by the nation that launched them with the identical or specific features such as those coins which are original.

2. Coins of a particular nation in ancient times are, in some cases, copied by another nation. An individual might believe that it is a forgery, however, it is not due to the fact that they would have been lawfully authorized in the nation where they came from.

3. Forgery could be related to a profit. It may be the primary goal of the counterfeiting syndicate. The federal government often utilizes forgery for a certain political propaganda, such as in the Second World War. The Germans created countless British and American banknotes for the intent of making money from them and destabilizing the opponent's financial circumstance.

4. Another recognized kind of fake coins are the replica coins. Replica merely suggests that the initial coins are copied with identical functions and markings. Nevertheless, the typical fake coins have their distinctions that can be found by professionals. Some deliberately place the word "copy" on the sides of the coins. The majority of these replicas are utilized for academic functions and museum displays.

5. The Lebanese connection is stated to have a big creation of fake coins. These coins were discovered to be utilized to trick lots of museums, business leaders, collectors and other nations which are looking for their ancient lost coins.

6. The circulated intended forgery and the collector intended forgery are kinds of forgeries where the coin worth is token intended, and the face values are accepted, despite their illegality and intrusive, unimportant values.

It is essential to see a professional to identify if the coin is fake. A common individual could quickly find the incorrect metal utilized for counterfeiting. If the individual is a collector of such products, he ought to be more familiar with these coins. A collector has to be more worried about the uncommon collectible coins due to the fact that this is where counterfeiters gain. They go for the really valuable market where they could make money.

Chapter 3.
How Can You Detect Counterfeit Gold Coins?

Coins are the basis of all developed countries, as physical currencies have become the primary means of conducting financial transactions. The ancient world relied on casting precious metals such as silver and gold into coins. This coin was used as a means of anointing trading machines and storing wealth for kings, emperors, and other rulers.

However, as long as the coins exist, counterfeiters have seen a great opportunity to make a property by making copies of low-value gold coins and passing them as real coins. Early counterfeiters created clay molds for the original coins and cast coins in similar shapes from metals such as gold. Gold coin counterfeiting was so widespread that strict laws were quickly enacted against it, often sentencing counterfeiters to death.

Over the years, counterfeiting technology has evolved into a popular method today. Plate or plate gold on cheap metal alloys to make almost perfect copies that are hard to find. Modern counterfeiters still rely on this method, but advances in alloying and plating methods have made great strides.

Fakeness in the modern world

You may be wondering why counterfeit coins still exist today. Most of the newly cast gold and silver coins are special promotional activities aimed at consumers seeking souvenirs of the bygone or specially regulated gold coins used for gold trading and investment.

For contemporary counterfeiters, the value of collecting and selling old gold coins as antiquities and pieces of art is immensely alluring.

How to find fake gold coins and avoid fraud?

As well as collecting gold coins, investing in gold sticks and coins is growing in popularity. People frequently consider gold to be one of the greatest and safest investments during times of crisis and economic turmoil. Scammers who offer to sell customers bogus gold coins at steep discounts are the last thing they want to be concerned about.

I want to give you a list of steps you can take to reduce the possibility of fraud and the acquisition of gold coins that are fake. Since coin counterfeiters have access to hundreds of more cutting-edge methods, this is by no means a comprehensive list. Even still, the majority of these items are inaccessible to the average person. If you want to make sure you are buying real gold coins of real value, be sure to follow the steps below.

Always buy gold coins from a registered and reputable dealer

You can lower your chance of acquiring fake gold coins by selecting a dealer or broker who is licenced to buy and sell gold coins and has a solid reputation in the community. This way, you can prevent receiving fake gold coins in the first place. Although there is little chance of fraud, there is no 100% guarantee that all registered traders will abide by the laws and refrain from engaging in counterfeiting. A warning sign should be raised if the dealer tries to persuade you to buy a certain gold coin or provides a special discount for no discernible reason. The other is when the dealer provides gold coins at a significant discount to the going rate.

Perform a Magnet Test on the Coins

Coins with a big percentage of gold will now no longer react to magnets considering that gold as treasured steel isn't prone to magnetic forces. Counterfeit gold coins regularly comprise less expensive metals that may be magnetized, so an easy magnet check is a clean manner to ferret out a scam. Modern counterfeiters use non-magnetic alloys while minting counterfeit cash, so a magnet check may not work on some occasions.

Examine the Mint Markings and Coin Details

This stage works best for those who are knowledgeable about the topic and are able to recognise the irregularities in gold coins that are fake. A specialist can easily identify the standard mint markings on genuine gold coins. Remember that counterfeiters do now no longer have the authentic molds used for casting the coins. Rather, they ought to use an actual gold coin as a version to create their casts. This regularly ends in a loss of element or inaccuracies that appear invisible at first glance, however, cannot fool an educated eye. If you're thinking about widespread funding for gold coins, do not forget to take a few to be inspected with the aid of using an educated expert. Modern gold coins adhere to strict policies and rules that decide their dimensions and weight. The variations are tiny and almost indistinguishable unless measured with expert equipment. With the usage of particular measuring equipment, it's easy to perceive essential variations as long as you know what you're looking for.

Compare the Price

One component that ought to have you ever walking for the hills is being supplied a tremendous deal on gold coin pricing. Anything with a first-rate distinction in fee is much more likely to be a capacity scam. There isn't any actual purpose for gold agents to provide gold coins at unique bargain costs for the reason that they make their dwelling from commissions.

Perform a Stack Test

To ensure that they are identical in terms of length, weight, and shape, gold coins that are produced by authorised, registered mints undergo a number of checks. An easy check you could carry out to test for consistencies in gold cash is the stack test. Take a handful of gold coins and begin stacking them on top of each other. Real gold coins ought to be clean to stack, developing a solid, balanced stack with no essential aesthetic variations.

If the stack appears unstable or the coins have uncommon bumps, slopes, or other weird elements, it is probably good to look at them closely or ask for an expert opinion before buying them.

Ping, ping, ping

The ping test is one of the earliest methods for detecting fake gold coins. In the past, specialists have noted that a gold coin makes a specific high-pitched ringing sound when it strikes a hard surface or another gold coin. Coins made of gold appear to ping for a longer period of time. Contrarily, fake coins are made of inferior metals that produce a muted, dull sound and a significantly shorter ringing when struck against a hard surface.

Relative density

Density testing is one of the most advanced techniques for distinguishing false from real gold. A lab and a tonne of equipment are required for the testing process, which may not be available to the common person. However, we believe that describing the process is essential.

A series of tests are performed when gold coins are submerged in water to ascertain their specific gravity. Coins made of gold should have a specific gravity of about 19.3. Your coins may be low-quality knockoffs if their specific gravity is much over or below the 19.3 threshold.

Assess conductivity

Since gold is frequently used in premium cables and conductors, it makes obvious that gold coins would be good heat and electrical conductors. Only ice cubes are needed for a straightforward conductivity test. Put ice cubes on the genuine gold coin and the alleged counterfeit coin. Ice cubes melt more quickly in gold coins than those made of inferior metal. Ice melts more quickly the higher the material's conductivity. You are welcome to use alternative methods to verify the authenticity of the gold coin on your own. Purchasing gold is one of the best decisions you can make. If you're wanting to diversify your portfolio or save money for retirement, gold is a terrific opportunity for long-term growth and financial security. Ensure that every test is logical and supported by reliable science. Licensed and recognized gold exchanges and brokers must be used when buying gold coins as an investment. To locate the gold exchange that best meets your needs browse the selection at Learn About Gold.

Today, there are ways to make money using pennies, but it's not a simple task. Purchasing ungraded coins, having them sorted, and then selling them for a profit is one strategy I've seen. However, you must use extreme caution while purchasing the coins. First, you need to be able to accurately grade a raw coin for yourself. Then you need to be able to buy the coin at least $20 below what it will sell for when graded, and that is assuming you're using the lowest price (longest turnaround time) for the grading service. If you are actually willing to take the time to buy the coins at the right price and then wait for them to be graded, then when you sell them, you can make a profit.

Another way to profit from coins is the most obvious. Buy them today at a good price, at or below the market price, and then hold them for several years until the market price moves up and then sell them.

Chapter 4.
Tips and mistakes to avoid when buying or selling coins

1. Do your research: Before buying or selling coins, it's important to thoroughly research the coin and the market. This will help you make informed decisions and avoid scams.

2. Use a reputable exchange: It's important to use a reputable exchange to buy and sell coins. Look for exchanges that have a good track record and are regulated by financial authorities.

3. Use a secure wallet: It's important to store your coins in a secure wallet, either on the exchange or on a personal device. This will help protect your coins from hacks and other security threats.

4. Be aware of fees: Exchanges and other platforms often charge fees for buying and selling coins. Be sure to understand the fees associated with your transactions to avoid any surprise costs.

5. Don't invest more than you can afford to lose: It's important to remember that the cryptocurrency market can be volatile, and the value of your coins may fluctuate significantly. Don't invest more than you can afford to lose.

6. Don't fall for scams: There are many scams in the cryptocurrency space, so it's important to be cautious. Don't send coins to unknown addresses, and be wary of any offers that seem too good to be true.

7. Don't forget to diversify: As with any investment, it's important to diversify your portfolio. Don't put all of your eggs in one basket by investing heavily in a single coin.

8. Take advantage of market trends: It's important to stay up to date on market trends and news. If you see a coin that is rising in value, it might be a good opportunity to buy. Similarly, if a coin is losing value, it might be a good time to sell.

9. Use stop-loss orders: A stop-loss order is a type of order that allows you to automatically sell a coin if it reaches a certain price. This can be useful for protecting yourself against significant losses if the value of a coin drops.

10. Don't let emotions guide your decisions: It's important to keep a level head when buying and selling coins. Don't make impulsive decisions based on fear or greed. Instead, try to stay rational and make decisions based on your research and analysis.

BOOK 4.
BEST CLEANING AND PRESERVING OF COINS

Chapter 1.
How to Take Care of Your Coins?

If you want to become a successful coin collector, you must take proper care of your coins. It takes a lot to take care of your coins in the real sense of the word. There are a few aspects that most people do not think about, but they are crucial to know. Take the time to understand how to properly care for your coins, as inappropriate maintenance can lower the number of your coins.

Handling Coins Correctly

Always treat collectible coins with care. When uncirculated coins are handled incorrectly, they might begin to wear, lowering their value. To keep your higher-grade circulated coins in the best condition possible, use the same care you would with your lower-grade coins.

Hand Sanitizer

Moisture coming out of your hands can chemically react with the coin's metal, causing damage that may not be seen for years. An additional need to wash your hands as anything present on your hands, such as dust, sweat, food debris, and grease, will be transmitted to the coin's surface.

These things can leave unappealing blemishes on your coin or, worse, cause it to start to wear. You should always grasp a coin between your thumb and index finger for almost the same purposes as earlier. While this isn't necessary for lower-grade circulation coins, it is a nice coin-care practice to develop.

Wear Gloves

Light cotton gloves will safeguard your coins if you can't wash your hands. When managing any valuable coin, some collectors wear them, although they are not required if your hands are dirt free and you hold the coin correctly.

Avoid eating or drinking while touching your coins or even anywhere near them. If these substances contact your coins, they may cause stains or color changes.

If you need to set a coin down after removing it from its holder, make sure it is on a hard floor, free from dust or any other material that might come into touch with it. A velvety pad is best, but a soft cloth or a dry sheet of Paper could serve for less precious things. Please avoid dragging or scraping your coins across any harsh surface.

Cleaning of Coins

Over time, coins can accumulate a lot of grime. Numerous strategies provide excellent cleaning solutions, whether you are trying to lighten up your old coins or put a sheen to make them valuable. Still, even before you continue, you should ask yourselves if you should wash your coins.

Wear a Mask

While wearing a mask is not strictly necessary, you should be conscious of what you are doing. When you breathe or talk, moisture from your mouth can get onto your coins without realizing it.

Keeping your coins in an airtight container with purified water and sand is a simple way to clean your regular pocket change. To brighten your money, simply seal the container and shake it firmly. This approach, however, depends on abrasion and is not recommended for precious, ancient, or collector coins.

Coin Cleaning

If you have collectibles or antique coins that you intend to sell or exchange in the years to come, you should seek professional counsel first. You don't want to dilute a coin's worth by cleaning it.

Nevertheless, if you only gather coins as a pastime and do not plan to sell or trade them, make them brilliant and shining. Coins collect germs as they pass from one person to another, so washing them will make handling them more sanitary. If a youngster is beginning a collection with ordinary circulation coins, you may also want to clean them to make the activity more sanitary for the child.

Submerge The Coin in Warm Water

This will allow the initial dirt buildup on your coin to be removed. Avoid any add-ons to raise the pressure, such as a jet, because the tap should have enough to get the job done. Holding a coin underneath the faucet for roughly one minute on either side is all that is required. Place them on a towel or rag once you are finished.

Water can be used to clean all coins. On the other hand, copper coins react to a wider range of substances than nickel or silver coins and hence cause environmental damage. This makes them more difficult to clean with water alone. Stop the drain before washing coins in your sink to avoid a coin falling from your hand and into the drain. Handle each coin independently so that the faucet can directly hit each coin.

Put The Coins in A Water-Soap Solution

In a small-sized bowl, take water from your tap and combine it with dish soap, then place each penny in the bath one at a time. Place the coin across your index and thumb and gently brush the dirt away from the face. The dirt would start to fall off now.

If you have an extremely filthy coin, soak it in the solution for a while. A non-abrasive liquid solvent, such as filtered water and a weak soap, will clean your coins effectively while containing no acids that could erode them.

Use a Soft Brush

While your coins are still in the soap and water solution, brush them. Brush the coin's face until it becomes shiny again. Rinse the coin frequently to avoid any scratches caused by dislodged dirt. When you do this too precious or antique coins, you risk leaving tiny scratches on them, lowering their value.

It is important not to touch the coin too aggressively. Concentrate your efforts on a small region and lightly brush it. Dry the coins by using a cloth. Make sure you dry every coin with a towel before storing it in a dry location. To avoid degrading your coins over time, ensure they are free of humidity before storing them. Your coins should be gleaming and lustrous. You will detect no residue if you use a cotton-free cloth. Touching the coins will prevent micro-scratches from being created by the material you are wiping them with.

Salt and Isopropyl Alcohol Bath

These substances are abrasive and acidic, and they will remove any dirt from your coin. In a dish, mix a cup of the over isopropyl alcohol with 2 tablespoons of salt to prepare your coin bath. Drop your coins in the solution after it has been mixed. Depending on how unclean your coins are, immerse them for between 2 hours to a week.

When soaking your coins, make sure you have a window open. Using distilled water, wash the pennies over your sink. With time, chemicals in tap water, such as chlorine, will damage your coins. After cleaning them, rinse them with purified water to ensure that any remaining chemicals are removed. All pollutants have been removed from distilled water. Distilled water can be purchased at a supermarket.

Allow the coins to air dry after dabbing them with a cloth. Repeat the process on the other side. To guarantee that your coins are completely dry, avoid stacking them shortly after drying. Allowing moisture to remain on the coin can cause it to deteriorate over time.

The coating of your coin might be affected by extreme temperatures. While they are drying, avoid exposing them to hot air. Blowing on the coin, not canned air, will remove any lint or dust left behind from patting your coins.

Store your coins in acid-free plastic-made folders at normal temperature. Cardboard, Paper and multiple plastics are prevalent storage materials that can cause harm over time. Any coin holder made of PVC should be avoided since it contains elements that might harm your coins. Intense temperatures or cold can destroy coins, so store them in an ambient temperature environment with low humidity.

Taking Care of Collectible Coins

Avoid storing your coins on a high, shaky shelf where they might fall over. Use a two-pocket box made of Polyester, designed specifically for storing coins, if you intend to display your coins on show.

Seek the advice of a Professional

Before cleaning your collectible coins, you should always speak with a competent coin grading service. Cleaning collectible coins can diminish their worth greatly; nevertheless, coin "toning," or the coloration and tarnishing caused by air exposure, can also contribute to its overall value. As a result, cleaning expensive or antique coins is not always recommended.

When holding ancient coins, typically grasp them on the edges rather than the face of the coin. Oils and fingerprints can depreciate the value of a coin. Because coin grading is regulated, even the tiniest blemish from swiping one-off can dramatically lower its worth.

Apply a layer of vaseline or any other lubricant using a cotton swab. Gently dab the coin with a specialized lint-free cloth until the lubricant is removed. This is a way to eliminate any undesired dirt or dust without affecting the coin's value. Use caution a magnifying glass with caution when doing this. Use a q-tip and a very delicate non-synthetic brush to apply the vaseline. Avoid smearing the coin with too much vaseline. The key is to apply the thinnest possible layer.

For 5 seconds, immerse coins in acetone. Putting any methanol on your coin can give them a brownish tint and drastically impair their value. Before leaving your coins to air dry, you must immediately rinse them with distilled water to remove all traces of acetone. Clean or rub your ancient coins only with a soft cloth. Since acetone is a solution rather than an acid, it will not devalue your coins until they are subjected to it for an extended length of time.

Acetone is a flammable substance. If you opt to use this chemical, use powder-free gloves. If you are using a distilled water jar, make sure the bottom is lined with a napkin so your coins do not get scratched when they touch inside the jar. Use acetone that is 100 percent pure. Other acetone-containing items will also include other compounds that will devalue your currency.

Keeping your Coins Safe

How would you keep your coins safe and secure now that you have them? We have spoken about handling coins safely to not get damaged. Now we must decide whether or not to maintain these coins in our possession and whether or not to do so again to protect them from danger.

Whether you have found some fine circulation coins or bought some from a reputable dealer, you will need a way to keep them safe from damage. There are a variety of ways that damage might occur. It is much more than getting 2 or even more, coins rub against one another in your Numismatics, which would be a no-no in and of itself. Scratches, nicks, and gouges are common effects of this type of damage, but your valuable coins can also be harmed in other ways.

Corrosion, fingerprints spots from atmospheric moisture droplets and dark toning are only a few types of deterioration in coin collecting. Natural fading on a silver coin, such as a bloom of champagne or gold color, can be magnificent. The damage we are talking about is commonly a result of a coin being exposed to specific air conditions or stored incorrectly. Maybe the proprietor tried cleaning it with a solvent not meant for coins. In any case, a coin can acquire an unattractive black or another dark color. Soaking such a coin frequently leads to additional deterioration.

Coin Damage and Coin Storage

Although most metals are generally durable, several circumstances might degrade the quality of your coins. Many coin collectors store their coins for extended periods without inspecting them. Regularly inspecting the state of your money in safekeeping is among the most effective strategies to prevent harm from occurring.

Humidity

The biggest enemy of a coin is humidity. Silver and copper coins are two of the most commonly utilized metals in coin manufacturing. Unfortunately, when these two metals come into touch with water, they react chemically. Water vapor is present in varying degrees everywhere around us, and it can penetrate almost anything. This is one of the most difficult environmental causes of coin damage.

Extremes of Heat and Cold

Heat does not always cause coins to corrode. On the other hand, heat shortens the time it would take for a coin to be harmed by other environmental conditions, including humidity, acids, and pollutants. Cooling can harm the fragile surface of unissued coins by condensing moisture into liquid water, which then deposits itself on the coin's surface.

Acids

Acids can be located in a variety of places. The most prevalent acid source is coin collection supplies made of regular Paper and cardboard that have had acid added to them during the manufacturing process. Over time, these chemicals will leak out of the paperboard, causing tarnishing and toning, particularly on silver and copper coins. Acids can be released by adhesives used in packaging. Wood furniture and common home products, including cleaning solutions and cooking gases, are acid sources. Do not put your coins in the same closet as cleaning materials or other chemicals.

Chlorine

Chlorine produces a chemical reaction in your coins that will degrade their appearance. Due to corrosion, this might range from mild ugly toning to pitting on the coin's surface. Flips manufactured of PVC-containing plastic are one of the main causes of this (polyvinyl chloride). Furthermore, gases from a steam room or pool can infiltrate into the space where your coin collection is kept.

Pollution in the Air

Air pollution is damaging to our wellness, but it is also dangerous to the condition of our coin collection. Air pollution is primarily a concern in densely populated regions, where the haze from automobiles can concentrate and infiltrate adjacent structures. Even though attempts have been made to limit the number of toxic gases automobiles generate, they can still present in sufficient quantities to destroy a coin. Avoid putting your coins near a driveway or a storage facility that stores petroleum materials.

Inappropriate Handling

The most avoidable type of coin damage is improper handling. Touching a coin with your hands can leave residues of chemicals and oils on the surface, causing it to weaken. Dropping a coin upon a solid floor can also inflict irreversible damage, lowering its value. Always use coin handling practices that are safe. This includes using soft cotton or nitrile gloves to handle your cash. Always use a soft cushion or towel to handle your coins.

Chapter 2.
Preserve and Protect the Collection

Coin Care and Cleaning

While it is good to maintain cleanliness in the surroundings, it is best not to clean the coins. A shiny coin may look nice, but maintaining its original appearance is essential for a collectible coin.

Cleaning the coin can reduce its numismatic value significantly. There are only a very restricted number of things you can do to improve a coin's appearance. You might harm it instead of enhancing it.

Unnecessary cleaning affects the value and cost of collectible coins. The patina on a coin is built up over the years and is part of its total essence and history and reflects a value much more than its face value. Remove it, and you can lessen its value by as much as 90%! Collectors value coins with attractive patinas, which, in effect, protect the coin's surface.

Like any work of art restoration, cleaning coins must be done by professionals. They know what techniques to employ that will work best and still have the coin as valuable as ever.

If you think that a tarnished coin you have just discovered needs to be cleaned, STOP! It is not a good idea. It is better to leave the coin alone. The color change you observe is a natural process called toning. And if allowed to progress by itself naturally and produce attractive results, it sometimes adds to the coin's value.

Toning is caused by the atoms' chemical reactions on the coin's surface, usually with sulfur compounds. It cannot be reversed, but "dips" in which strip molecules from the coin's surface are available. Bear in mind, however, that professionals should only do this.

You need to observe several rules when considering cleaning the coins you have obtained, found, bought, or inherited.

1. Never clean a coin that you do not know the numismatic value. If you doubt if it's valuable or not, then don't clean it either. It is best to leave coins the way you found them, untouched. Erring on the conservative side is preferable to ruining the coin for nothing. Store them in holders made for the purpose. Coin collectors and dealers prefer coins in their original condition, so do not attempt to alter their state. Cleaning will probably ensure more harm than good.

2. Because you are not supposed to clean the coins yourself, you need to take the coins to a professional coin cleaning service. They use a technique called "dipping" that will properly clean the coins without reducing their value. This is important, especially if the coin's date and details cannot be determined because of corrosion. A professional will know how to avoid or minimize further damage to the coin.

3. In the situation that you must clean the coin, you have found, then do it with the least harmful method. Do not use harsh chemicals, sulfuric acid, polishing cloth, vinegar, abrasive pastes, or devices that give a smooth and shiny result on the coin. Experiment first with lesser value coins before coins with high value.

4. Cleaning is a big issue in coin collecting, so you have to disclose this fact to a buyer if you are selling a coin that you know has been cleaned.

Soaking Coin

Cleaning Different Types of Coins

- **Uncirculated coins** – should never be cleaned at all because cleaning will ruin any mint luster.

- **Gold Coins** – should be cleansed cautiously in neat, lukewarm bubbly purified liquid consuming a cottony fiber wash-down fabric or an incredibly easy tooth scrub. Gold is smooth metal, so you should take extra care to avoid disfiguring or scratching.

- **Silver Coins** – valuable silver coins should not be cleaned at all. The blue-green or violet oil-like tarnish, dirt, minerals, or other residues some silver coins have enhances their appearance and should be left alone. Dark silver coins must be cleaned with ammonia, rubbing alcohol, vinegar, or polish remover with acetone. Do not rub or polish them.

- **Copper Coins** – if necessary to clean them, soak them in grape oil. If not available, olive oil will do. Never attempt to rub them in any way. However, getting results may take several weeks to a year, so be patient.

- **Nickel Coins** – best cleaned with warm, soapy distilled water using a soft toothbrush. If cleaning badly stained nickel coins, use ammonia diluted 3 to 1 with distilled water.

How to Store Your Coins

You need to actually store your coins properly to avoid giving them any scratch to reduce their numismatic value. You need to use the proper type of holder, depending on the value of the coin you are storing.

There are folders and albums available commercially that you can purchase for storing your series or type collection. When using paper envelopes, make sure that their materials are especially suited for holding coins, especially the high-value ones, since sulfur or other chemicals present in the paper can cause a reaction and change the coin's color.

Plastic flips made of mylar and acetate are good materials for long-term storage, but since they are hard and brittle, they may scratch the coin if they are not inserted and removed carefully. "Soft" flips used to be created after polyvinyl chloride (PVC), which decayed after some time and imparted grievous ends aimed at the coinages. PVC gave an emerald look on the pennies. PVC reverses are certainly no longer manufactured and marketed in the US.

Tubes can hold several same size coins and are seemingly for the majority space of distributed coinages and higher-grade coins if they are not moved. For more valuable coins, use hard plastic holders as they do not contain harmful materials and can protect coins against scratches and other physical damage.

Collectible Coins in Their Cases

For more valuable coins, you can opt to use slabs as they offer good protection. Slabs are hermetically sealed hard plastic holders for individual coins. However, one drawback is the expense involved, and you will not be able to get at the coin easily if there is a need to do so.

For long-term storage, a dry environment without significant temperature fluctuation and low humidity is important. You need to minimize exposure to moist air, as this will cause oxidation. It may not reduce the coin's value, but reducing oxidation will help the coin look more attractive. To control atmospheric moisture, you need to place silica gel packets in the coin storage area.

You still need to check on your collection periodically, even if you store them in a safety deposit box. If not stored properly, problems could develop, and you can do something about it before any serious damage occurs.

Protecting Your Collection from Loss by Fire of Theft

There will always be the threat of loss by fire or theft to any of your properties. However, just as you would protect your house or car from them, there are some precautions you can take to minimize them. Bear in mind that most homeowner insurance excludes coins and other items of numismatic value from coverage. You can usually get a rider, however, but for an additional premium payment.

You can also obtain a separate policy. Consider joining the American Numismatic Association (ANA) that offers insurance for their members' coin collections. Be sure that you have a catalog of your collection stored separately from the coins. Note where you have obtained each coin, the coin's condition, and the price you paid for it.

Taking individual close-up pictures of each coin is also a good idea. Get an appraisal from a professional who uses a Blue Book or Red Book for this purpose. The insurance company will need the documents of the appraisal.

Safes protect against theft, fire, dust, water, or other environmental factors that could damage your possessions. For your coins, they offer relative protection. Some safes provide adequate protection from fire but are not suitable for theft protection.

Some safes do deter thieves but are not fireproof. Your collection can be damaged or destroyed by fire even if the flames do not touch your coins. The heat may be extreme enough to melt them.

Another concern when storing your coins in a safe is the level of humidity. A high level will cause oxidation, which is bad for the coins. The ideal level is 30% relative humidity (RH). The RH inside the safe is dependent on the ambient RH where the safe is located. Most modern safes, fortunately, are adequately insulated and are constructed with good seals. Silica gel packets can help reduce humidity.

So, if you opt to keep your collection at home, see that you get a home safe that provides enough fire and humidity protection and protection against theft. Make sure you take measures to prevent or dissuade a burglar from invading your home. Adequate lighting and secure, strong locks are recommended. You can ask law enforcement officers for more valuable tips.

One way of protecting your investment against theft is to be discrete about being a coin collector. The information you divulge about yourself to many people may eventually reach the wrong person. Having all numismatic-related promotional materials sent to a post office box instead of your home may help.

Chapter 3.
Main Causes of Coin Damages

You might easily tamper with your coins before realizing it. Coin collectors enjoy bragging about their collections to certain other coin enthusiasts and close friends. However, it's also likely that your behavior and the way you display the coins could be hurting them. Even professional coin dealers have been caught unknowingly spitting upon their coins, in my experience.

Spend some time learning how to handle, clean, preserve, and safeguard your expensive coins if you really want to secure the investment you are putting in the coin collection. If not, until you or the successors decide to sell them, the value of the coin collection would be significantly lower.

Your Coins Being Touched

Your coins could be harmed just by coming into contact with bare skin. High-grade collectible coins are particularly vulnerable to damage from finger contact. If your fingers get into touch with mint state & Proof coins, you run the risk of damaging your coins. Various oils, acids, & microscopic sand on your fingers will stick to the coins' surfaces and create discoloration or microscopic scratches. Wear wool, Nitrile, or latex mittens when handling coins, & only handle the corners.

If someone drops the coins on a solid floor, they may potentially be harmed. Put the coins above a soft pad or cloth result while handling them. When you're done, put the coins back in the appropriate coin holder.

Purify Your Coins

Cleaning or shining the coins will not improve their condition, with the exception of coins that have just been pulled out from the ground during a metal detecting search. It is normal for metal to oxidize or tone once it has been exposed to the air. If you remove this fading, the coin will further lose any existing mint luster but also seem harsh and unpleasant, as well as develop microscopic abrasions which will reduce its grade. Coins that have retained their natural toning are valued far beyond coins that have lost it.

The study of numismatics has a field called coin conservation. The molecular texture of the coin over the base is not altered or removed during coin conservation, unlike coin cleaning. In other terms, proper maintenance will eliminate impurities from the coin's surface without affecting or removing even one metal molecule. If you must, be careful when cleaning coins.

Spitting on the Coins

Just as damaging as handling or cleaning your coins is talking about them. Particles of saliva that fall from the mouth as you converse will settle on the coins if you leave them exposed while chit-chatting. These tiny salivary flecks can leave behind spots & discolorations which are challenging to get rid of. This is how these uncirculated, Evidence, & mint state coins have been damaged by collectors. You can talk about the coin collection all you want; just ensure the coins are out of the way when you do.

Shake Off Their Holders

By withdrawing the mint set, commemorative coins, Proof set, or encapsulated coins from the holders the mint issued for them, you are assured of significantly reducing their value. The holders, including the box as well as any accompanying literature, make up the "set" and must be preserved in perfect condition.

The value of coins in its protective casings that were slabbed by a 3rd party grading service is similar. Never take a coin out of one of these permanent containers unless you have a good cause, too, such as to break out of its block. Before 1955, certain early sets, however, were packaged in paper wrappers which contained polymers or acids that deteriorate over time. You should take these coins out of their respective holders while they sustain any harm.

Bring the coins to a reputable coin dealer/coin show & ask for advice if you're not sure what else to do. In sequence for you to receive the greatest dollar for the collection, a trustworthy coin broker will offer you advice. It's

Introduce Acid to Them

Coins kept in paper packets can spoil your collection. If you don't take care to use acid-free paper, keeping the coins in document envelopes or storage boxes is a surefire way to wreck them. As the material degrades over time, acidic chemicals are released into the air near your coins. Your shiny, genuine mint exterior coins will experience spotting, discoloration, and possibly even oxidation (toning) due to this acid. Always make sure to get acid-free cardboard and paper when stocking up on items for coin storage.

Finally, if you decide to store the coins on acid-free paper items, be sure to keep them in a space with a low relative humidity level. Paper is formed of biological material, which will eventually degrade, particularly in a climate with a lot of humidity. Here on paper, mold & mildew can grow and produce acids which will eat away at the face of the coins.

Put Some Green Slime on Your Coins

Storing the coins inside PVC-based plastic flaps, holders, or boxes is another effective technique to create spots and cause the face of the coins to deteriorate. Your coins may eventually become harmed by the chemical residue of some plastics, much like how the acid inside the paper may destroy them. The coins may quickly develop a sticky green coating over their faces if you store them in convenient food-grade plastic boxes or soft, flexible coin flips that will irreversibly harm them. Keep an eye out on coins & sets that come in PVC coin carriers and were produced by mints all over the world. Before they sustain any damage, the coins in these holders should be swiftly removed.

Exposing Them to Dangerous Things

Your coins will deteriorate if you keep them in a cellar or attic. If you keep the coins in the loft or cellar, you are undoubtedly subjecting them to temperature and relative humidity fluctuations that will hasten acid formation or encourage oxidation.

Additionally, the containers used to store your coins (including flips, paper envelopes, paper holders, containers, etc.) may degrade quickly under these circumstances. It is preferable to keep the coin collection in the dark, damp, and temperature-controlled space, like a locked box or specialist coin cabinet, to keep it secure.

BOOK 5.
GENERATING PROFIT WITH COINS

Chapter 1.
Need to Know Before Investing in Coin Collection

Before making investments in coin collection, there are certain things you need to get acquainted with for everything to go smoothly. The following are some tips to get you started with investing in collectible coins.

1. Understand the factors that add to a coin's value

The best investment you can make while starting up your coin collection is the investment of time. The first thing you should actually do is to carefully make research on the collectible coin industry to get more knowledge about the factors that contribute to a coin's value and the things you should actually look out for when making your collection. For instance, you should find out things about the following areas when making research on a new coin:

- The source of its numismatic value (the reason why collectors find it valuable and its history)
- The year it was minted
- The location at which it was minted
- The coin's condition
- The melt value of the coin.

Of course, you can never be certain that a particular coin will appreciate over some time. Just carry out your research and make investments on only the items you're willing to put your money into.

2. Make purchases from trusted companies (or get in touch with your physical sellers)

Making purchases from just any online is a test of luck. Instead of hoping that the item you purchased is exactly as you imagined it to be and in the end, you get something different, find yourself a reputable company who have the reputation of making sales of high-quality collectible coins to interested buyers. For instance, if you have been trying to purchase the 2020 Silver Eagle Coin, try to find companies like SD Bullion which provides security for a buyer when investing in collectible coins.

If you would rather purchase your coins from other sellers who are not well-established, you should meet up with the person physically to completely analyze the condition of the coin and make sure you're not being ripped off. After you have examined the coin, try to get a second opinion so that you can confirm the true value of the coin.

When it comes to purchasing collectibles, you can never be too careful!

3. Look out for potential red flags that point to a scam

Just as is the case with most valuable items, there would always be people who'd like to make money off them the wrong way. While trying to make purchases on valuable items, be sure to actually look out for red flags such as a dealer who behaves cunningly and won't let you see the paperwork or the condition of the coin before making your purchase, documents that seem edited and do not have the proper grading information, cases that seem opened, higher prices than the quality of the item, and false claim about being able to buy back an item. If you notice any of these things while making transactions with a coin dealer, you should probably check somewhere else.

4. Make investments in tools required to keep your coins in mint condition

Most collectible coins are only able to keep up their value if they are in mint condition. If your coin is not handled properly and gets slightly damaged, you could lose some amount from the first investment you made.

See to it that your coins are kept in a cool, dry place, do not throw away their original cases (or get a new one if you've lost them), and keep all documents about the coin somewhere it can't get damaged. Going over these steps would help you keep your coins safe and protect your investment.

5. Expand your collection of collectible coins

Just as you would like to expand your portfolio of stocks, it is also important to expand your coin collection to cut down risks while making investments. This implies expanding your investment across classic coin offerings, rare coins, gold and silver bullion, and other common products collectors find interest in. It is not guaranteed that all the coins will retain their value after some years; it is advised that you make your collection on a wide variety of valuable, rare coins so you're sure to build a perfect collection that would earn you lots of money when you sell in the future.

Chapter 2.
How to Sell Your Coins

The following are steps to guide you while making sales on your coin collection:

Valuing Coins

1. Identify the coin: Before making a coin sale, you should have some details and information about your coin. You can type them into an online search engine to discover the kind of coin you have.

   • You should also be able to get help from coin dealers and collectors. Take a clear picture of the two sides of the coin and send it to the coin dealer or collector if you can't take it to them in person.

2. Learn about the condition of the coin: The condition of a coin is a very important factor that determines how much it's worth. Check to see if there are any blemishes or scratches. The more damaged your coin is, the less value it's worth. You should also check to find printing errors since they often increase the value of the coin.

   • Coins have a grading scale of 0-70 where 0 indicates a "Poor" condition and 70 indicates "Mint Condition."

   • Be sure, not to clean the coin yourself even if you find them dirty. Coins are historical artifacts and collectors like to collect them just the way they are. Cleaning the coin can damage it further.

3. Check for the value of the coin: After you have identifies the kind of coin you have at your actual disposal, the next thing to do is estimate how much it's worth. You can find various sites online that can give you a list of the current values of coins. Other

than visiting sites, you can also go to a local bookstore to ask for "The Official Red Book," here you should be able to find a very detailed list of coin values.

- The coins are listed at wholesale price. You might not get as much pay when you sell the coins individually.

4. Monitor auctions to learn about the worth of your coin: Another method you can use to get information on the value of your coin is by searching recent sales. You can find all kinds of coin from sites such as Heritage Auctions. Look out for coins similar to the one you own to have an idea of how much people pay for them.

- Find an appraiser to value your coin collections: Appraisers are very important when you want to make sales on valuable coins or a large collection
- Check for online feedback from other customers or consult the Better Business Bureau to investigate the reputation of the appraiser.
- A lot of respectable dealers are parts of groups such as the American Numismatics Association or Professional Coin Grading Services. You can find trustworthy appraisers on these sites.

5. Sort coins according to value: Different buyers like to focus on different kinds of coins. If you're making sales on multiple coins at the same time, it's best to sort them into value-based groups. Separate the groups into high, medium, and low-value coins. You can group the coins in whichever method you like, but grading by wholesale value is the easiest way to grade the coins.

- You can also choose to sort the coins based on how worn they are, the metals used to make them, or where they were printed.

Finding Buyers

1. Talk to reputable coin dealers: The most natural places you can go to when making sales on coins are local coin dealers. This is where low and medium-value coins are usually sold. Whenever you visit a coin dealer, check out their stock to see if they have a coin collection similar to the one you're about to sell to them, chances are they'll give you a fairer price.

- A lot of dealers like to find rare coins, but you'll usually get more money if you sell these coins at auctions or private collectors.
- Bear in mind that these dealers run businesses. To make a profit, they'll have to pay you at a price lower than the wholesale price.
- The best thing to do is allow a couple of dealers to evaluate your coins. Stay polite while shopping around.

2. Go to coin shows: When you go to coin shows you'll be able to meet with a lot of buyers and sellers. Try to meet people that deal with the same kind of coins as you. Conclude on a fair selling point, but don't be in a hurry to sell your coins. You might not always get fair deals at coin shows, but you'll have the chance to meet trustworthy dealers and people who can guide you on the right path.

3. Find coin collector magazines: Publications such as Numismatic News and Coin World help to advertise coin dealers. While magazines provide you with information about coin sales, they also recommend perfect buyers for your coins. You can find these magazines in local coin shops or through sites online.

- Whatever you do, be sure not to let local newspapers advertise your coins for you as this could attract thieves.

4. Take the coins to auctions: Coin auctions can be carried out both in person and on online platforms. They come in actual different sizes and can be local, regional, or national. Try to auction with coins similar to the ones you have, such as copper or silver. It is impossible to predict auctions, so there's a chance that you might earn less than what a dealer would pay for it or you might earn higher than your sale price.

   - Buyers and sellers would have to pay a fee of around 10-15% of the final sale price to the Auctions.
   - Auction sites such as eBay are also very good, but you should be wary of fraud.

Handling Sales

1. Pick the buyers that give you fair analysis: Unscrupulous buyers propose low offers at first bid with the hope of getting a good deal in the end. Watch the buyer closely while he evaluates the coin if you can. All the coins should be analyzed one after the other. Try not to make deals with anyone that offers you a flat price without even making out time to analyze the coins carefully. Do not agree to sell coins to anybody that pressures you into selling your coins quickly.

   - Find dealers that have been flagged with position reviews and feedback from popular numismatics organizations.

2. Have many buyers evaluate your coins: Be sure to actually shop around to get the best deals for your coins. Visit a lot of dealers and have them make their evaluations on your coins and make offers on them. Give your opinion on every one of the dealers' offers and tell them you'll meet with them later. Choose the dealer that gave the best deal or the one you're most comfortable doing business with.

3. Sell the entire collection as a whole: When making sales on a collection of coins, the best thing to actually do is to keep the coins as a package deal. Most dealers might not want to purchase the entire collection, they are most likely going to pick the ones with the highest values and leave the ones with less value and they are more difficult to sell. Set a price for the collection and stick to it.

4. Document your sales: Even if you get a coin for free you can still be landed into legal problems for it. Your government probably takes taxes from the profit you make from selling coins. For this reason, you should always keep a document of all the coin sales you make as well as any coin purchases.

   • Go to your local tax laws to find ways how to report your income.

Chapter 3.
Top Websites for Coin Collectors and Enthusiasts

A great resource for learning about coins and coin collecting is the internet. Unfortunately, the Internet is also the biggest source of false information worldwide. These top coin-related websites were chosen based on the information they provide and their accuracy of it. You will also be able to select from a selection of sites that will provide you with the most information and knowledge.

Mint of the United States

All of the currently offered mint goods are accessible in the shopping area. Typically, the mint will only sell coins and medals currently being manufactured. Things from a year ago that haven't been sold yet may still be on the market. You must visit your preferred coin shop or browse online if you're looking for older coins.

The United States Mint's very early beginnings, how coins are made, and other details about the mint and its fascinating history are all covered in the history and learning area.

CoinFacts by PCGS

One of the most thorough websites on practically every issue of American coins ever made is PCGS CoinFacts. The United States Mint's pattern coins are also covered in great depth, as are colonial, private, and territory issues. Every sort of coin has a link on the homepage, making it simple to explore the website.

You can access an overview of a specific coin type by clicking on one of the type coin titles. Additionally, PCGS CoinFacts offers top-notch images of each coin type and subtype.

You can find specific information for a given coin by clicking on the individual links. To see the intricate intricacies of each coin, click on the crisp photos. Detailed parameters include designer, diameter, weight, and mintage. Detailed demographic reports, price lists, and recent auction results reveal the information.

Newman Numismatic Portal

Eric P. Newman, a renowned coin collector in the field of numismatics, donated to establish the Newman Numismatic Portal. Newman became one of the most renowned researchers in the field of coin collecting thanks to his fascination with coins and unquenchable curiosity. Newman started to sell his coin collection in 2013. His sale generated millions of dollars in revenue. This money was partly contributed to support the Washington University in St. Louis, Missouri, which hosts the numismatic research site.

The Newman Numismatic Portal contains resources for all levels of numismatists, including those who are just starting. Additionally, almost 100,000 coin collecting-related books and journals have been digitally preserved and made completely searchable.

CoinNews.net

A selection of numismatic articles and coin-collecting pricing calculators may be found on the CoinNews website. One of the best brand-new coin-collecting websites is this one. Daily updates to the website include breaking news and relevant information for coin collectors. The U.S. Mint, international mints, news affecting bullion prices, coin shows, and auctions are all covered on this website.

The website offers coin-collecting tools that any coin collector would find helpful in addition to the current news issues. Although not every coin type ever produced by the

United States Mint is covered, the extensive information on contemporary coins and more well-known series will aid you as you actually embark on your coin collecting journey. Most Canadian and Australian coins are in the globe coin division. This is a comprehensive list of information for world coin collectors. A calculator for inflation, a currency converter, and current bullion prices are also available on the website.

World Price Guide for NGC

The NGC World Price Guide is among the world's most reliable price guides. The prices of all coins around the globe from 1600 to the present are available in this completely searchable database.

This comprehensive guide to world coin values was produced in collaboration with NumisMaster from Krause Publications and NGC. Krause-Mishler catalog numbers are used to organize the data, which contains coin values, photographs, and details like weight, composition, bullion value, artist/engraver, and edge type. All users have free and open access to the information.

Before beginning your search, you must know the origin nation, area (if any), and denomination. Any coins that fit your search parameters will have their images and overview information shown on a selection page once you do an open-ended search. You can access the database's specific pricing information if you know the date and/or catalog number.

Heritage Auctions

Heritage Auctions, situated in Dallas, Texas, is the biggest numismatic auction house in the world. Additionally, Heritage has locations throughout Asia, Europe, and the United

States. Heritage was founded in 1976 and offered a comprehensive selection of rare coins, fine and decorative art, sports memorabilia, and other high-quality items.

Heritage is the top seller of precious and rare coins, but the average collector can also buy reasonably priced objects for their collection. Their accessible database contains comprehensive information, catalog descriptions, and values realized for more than two million coin auction records. Their entire catalog of auctions is available online. However, be aware that a 20% "buyers fee" and shipping costs will be added to the final amount on your invoice.

You can also sell your coins through Heritage. The "seller's charge" is adjustable but often represents a commission of roughly 15%. Consigning a single coin or your complete collection won't be worthwhile unless you anticipate getting at least $5,000 to $10,000 in return at auction.

Great Collections

To service the rare coin and bullion community, Ian Russell created GreatCollections as a brand-new coin auction business in 2010. His extensive knowledge of Tele-Trade coin auctions offered him a unique viewpoint that allowed him to establish an online coin auction business that caters to novice and experienced coin collectors.

Regardless of the value of the coin, professional photographs are provided. One of the lowest buyer's fees of any online auction is only 10%, with a minimum of $5 per coin. The "seller's fee" is not imposed by Great Collections. Additionally, fully searchable, its database of auction results offers several choices to assist you in focusing your search on a certain coin of interest.

Mint Error News

Mint Error News is your website if you're interested in mint mistakes. The editor/publisher and CEO of Mike Byers Inc. He has over actual 35 years of experience as a professional numismatist and is a world authority on error coins.

The website's main attraction is the free and fully downloadable Mint Error News Magazine. Each issue is jam-packed with the latest finds, full-color images, and comprehensive educational content for error coin collectors.

A glossary of coin error phrases, an online museum of coin faults with high-resolution pictures, and a price guide to help you estimate the value of your mint error coin are just a few of the many online features available on the website. Mint Error News welcomes stories, discoveries, and images of certified major mint errors from all collectors and dealers for evaluation and publishing.

Association for American Numismatics

To assist you in your coin collecting endeavors, the largest coin club in the world has a newly renovated and cutting-edge website. Five individuals devoted to the hobby of coin collecting created the American Numismatic Association (ANA) in 1891. With information to support coin collectors worldwide, the ANA maintains one of the largest online presences more than 125 years later.

Every coin collector can find something at the ANA, from joining a coin club or locating a dealer to attending a seminar. Virtual tours of the ANA Money Museum, unique tools, and materials for young collectors are all included. The Numismatist, the ANA's monthly publication, is available in digital format to association members.

Kitco Bullion Prices

Numerous coins are made of precious metals, significantly impacting the coin's worth. The cost of precious metals may change drastically during erratic market activity. This could increase a coin's value as bullion over its market value as a collectible coin. This website will provide you with historical and current spot values for gold, silver, platinum, palladium, and rhodium if you're interested in investing in bullion coins.

BOOK 6.
THE RAREST COINS IN THE WORLD AND IN AMERICA

Chapter 1.
How to Find Rare Coins

Finding error coins in your daily pocket change can be both entertaining and lucrative, and it's a simple process. Develop good coin-checking habits from the start, and you might come across some circulating error coins and die varieties. Visit a coin show or a coin store and search through the dealer's inventory for mistakes and kinds she could have missed for a greater challenge. Many more discoveries yet to be discovered. Some of them will be minor items with a low numismatic value. Furthermore, you may come across a major mint error that's worth a lot of money. Finally, keep in mind that you should base your expectations on what is currently trending. To put it another way, valuable error coins can be found, but they are valuable because they are uncommon. Everyone would do it if they could go to the bank, get a few rolls of coins to search through, and pull out a few hundred dollars worth of rare coins. As a result, they would not be uncommon. It's not uncommon to go through ten, twenty, or even thirty rolls of coins and come up empty-handed.

You can detect rare and flawed coins in circulation with the help of the resources listed below:

- Loupe or magnifying glass. A 5x to 10x power was recommended.
- An incandescent bulb, a good desk lamp
- A soft pad or cloth
- Your daily pocket money (or purchase coin rolls to search!)

Examine your coins in groups of similar coins whenever possible. Check all of your pennies first, then your nickels, and finally your dimes. After the first couple of coins, your eye will become accustomed to seeing each type, allowing you to quickly scan them.

The more dramatic the error or variation, the higher its value. You can always get rolls of coins from your local bank if you don't have enough pocket change to dig through. When you examine coins in groups of similar types, you are also more likely to notice differences between them. Don't get bogged down in the details! It's usually not worth much if the doubling or other flaw is so minor that it's difficult to see with a 10x loupe. Look for anything unexpected or unusual in the lettering. Only a portion of a word is doubled on many doubled die variants. Abrasion, polishing, or greasy dirt on the die face can cause letters to strike incorrectly on the coin. Turn the coin over and over again, examining it from various perspectives. In the inscriptions, look for missing letters, doubling, and other oddities.

Because the date and mintmark are among the most valuable errors, you're likely to find in circulation, you should pay special attention to them. Check to see whether any outmoded coins landed up in your change as you are going through this collection of coins. Indian Head pennies and Buffalo nickels, for instance, have been discovered by certain people today. Additionally, watch out for coins that have been altered to mimic real mint faults. Take your find to a coin exhibition or a dealer if you're unsure so they can evaluate it. A tip that's going to save: Do not turn the coin over to check the mint mark or date if it is on the reverse side (or the edge, as on Presidential Dollars). Wait until the reversal, but when it's time, double-check everything. To check for are die cracks, cuds, and missing components. Look for doubling in the chin, lips, ears, and eyes of the portrait. Additionally, keep an eye out for anything unusual on the rim.Check each coin with caution. Some unscrupulous individuals will try to deceive you by altering genuine US coins to make them appear to be error coins. Someone could, for example, cut a coin in half with a hacksaw to make it look like an error coin. As your understanding of coins increases, you'll be able to recognise manipulated coins apart from genuine mint mistakes. From top to bottom, gently and painstakingly flip the coin (not side-to-side). If the coin was right-side-up before being turned over, the reverse should be the same way. Because the United States Mint takes great care to ensure that die rotation on its coins is correct, coins that are significantly out of rotation are considered moderately valuable error coins. Make it a habit to check the rotation of each coin you handle. The 180-degree rotation errors are the most valuable of all, so don't overlook them! Examine the reverse side of the coin in the same way you did the obverse, but this time with the coin upside down. Look for any doubling, missing elements, or other oddities in the inscriptions and devices Pay particular attention to the coin's mint mark if one is there. To help you see details more clearly, try tilting the coin at various angles in relation to the light. Examine the edge of your coin as the last step in the inspection process. Roll the coin along your palm to see the entire edge while keeping an eye out for seams, lines, missing reeded edges, and other abnormalities. Look for doubled or missing letters if the edge has letters.

Chapter 2.
The Rarest American Coins

Over the years, the United States has come up with some of the world's most valuable coins. The following are actually some of the most valuable coins in the United States based on their value at the moment and the ability of the collector to find them in uncirculated/mint condition.

1. 1913 Liberty Head Nickel

Just a few years ago, the 1913 Liberty Head Nickel was sold at an auction for an impressive sum of $3.1 million. However, the value of this coin can be placed at $4.4 million.

2. 1870 Silver Dollar

Sometimes called the Seated Liberty, the 1870 Silver Dollar has turned out to be one of the most revered coins in the world. One of these coins in mint condition can be purchased at a price of about $2.1 million lighter.

3. 1927 Double Eagle (D)

Not everyone would like to spare an amount of $1.2 million but coin enthusiasts with the funds would get the 1927 D Double Eagle.

4. 1794 Silver Dollar

If you're looking to invest $825, 098, well look no further than the 1794 Silver Dollar, that's if you're able to find one of the very few pieces produced.

5. 1838 Half Dollar (O)

During the time of the coin's mintage, there was an outbreak of yellow fever in New Orleans together with some other complications with the coins press and so the U.S. Mint was only able to produce about 12 pieces. The 1838 Half Dollar is now valued at about $745, 000 USD.

Chapter 3.
The Rarest Coins Worldwide

The average lifespan of a circulating coin is 30 to 40 years, although some fortunate collectors have discovered coins from the mid-1900s in their pocket money. There are still certain coins in circulation that date back to earlier times in American history that have been sold for thousands of dollars at auction.

Coins throughout the 1930s had a 90% silver and 10% copper composition. For both collectors and smelters, this composition is what makes these coins valuable. Because of this, you must look at the coins that are in the best shape while examining those that are worth the highest. Although it is illegal to melt down US currency, the value of the silver itself determines a coin's basic worth.

Listed below are some of the rarest coins that are still in circulation:

1. 1969-S Lincoln Cent with a Doubled Die Obverse

This is actualy one of the rarest coins in the world. The Secret Service took possession of the specimens that were first made until the United States Mint admitted that they were authentic. Counterfeits abound but are usually imprinted with the wrong mint mark. Back in May 2014, a single mom in Texas came across the coin while going through rolls of coins.

Approximate value: Around $40,000 or more in AU-50.

2. 1970-S Small Date Lincoln Cent with a Doubled Die Obverse

Just as is the case with all true doubled die varieties, just a single side of the coin displays doubling. If the two sides show doubling on any part of the coin, the coin probably gives off-strike doubling instead and is valued less than a true doubled die.

Approximate value: Around $3,500 in Ef-40.

3. 1972 Lincoln Cent with a Doubled Die Obverse
4. 2004-D Wisconsin State Quarter with an Extra Leaf

A variety of experts have different opinions about the cause and long-term value of this coin, but it has been included in the list due to its accessibility in pocket change and its value at the moment.

Something to note is that there should only be actually one leaf hanging on the left side of the ear of corn.

If by chance, you find two leaves hanging to the left, then it's a rare and valuable error coin.

Approximate value: $200 to $300 in MS-60.

5. 1999 Wide "Am" Reverse Lincoln Cent

This variety has been known to be existence for 3 dates, 1998, 1999, and 2000, with 1999 being the rarest of them all.

The mint mistakenly used a proof die to strike regular circulation coins.

Approximate value: $5 to $25 during periods of circulation, $75 to $600 in MS-63 or better depending on color. 1999 comes up with the top prices followed by 2000.

6. 1982 No Mint Mark Roosevelt Dime

Back in the years, the United States used to produce these coins, after which the coin dies would be transferred to the individual branch mints for punching with the right mint mark letter before being shipped off. This variety is usually made with one or more punched dies.

Approximate value: About $30-$50 in AU-50, more for actual higher grades.

7. Presidential Dollar Edge Lettering Errors

Ever since the first Presidential Dollar was issued back in the year 2007, some errors have been observed with the lettering on the edge of these coins. The edge lettering is imprinted on the coin after the coin is struck. In some cases, it is completely left out. In some others, the edge lettering has already been placed there several times.

Approximate value: $50 to $3000, depending on the President in charge.

8. 1995 Doubled De Obverse Lincoln Cent

This doubled-die variety came up with several mainstream interests at the time it was used as the cover story in USA Today. Specimens have been found in recent times.

Approximate value: About $20-$40 in uncirculated condition.

9. Silver Half Dollars

A lot of people believe that the silver in the United States coins was stopped back in 1964, but that's a lie. The Half Dollar coin was imprinted with silver right until the year 1970.

Most people use the Half Dollars to purchase items from 1965 to 1970 or sell them off in rolls of halves they take to the bank, forgetting that they are at least 40% silver.

Approximate value: About $20

Uncirculated State Quarters

Just as the state of the economy has been diminishing, people who kept rolls of Quarters for a long time have been spending them into circulation. If you're able to gather whole rolls of uncirculated quarters of some in-demand states, you should get as much as $30 for each roll.

Approximate value: $20-$52 per roll for actually and strictly uncirculated rolls of certain states.

Chapter 4.
Tips for Safely Buying and Selling Rare Coins

Several elements go into determining a coin's value, and unless you're a seasoned coin collector or an expert numismatist, you might not be aware of them. When a professional analyzes a coin, two coins that seem identical on the surface might have dramatically different values. A tiny change in the year, location of production, or grade of a coin may often mean the difference between hundreds of dollars.

Evaluate and Organize

Yes, you can just take the whole stack, bag, or box of scattered coins to a coin trader and have them sort them out and give you an approximation. However, it's helpful to know if you are coping with such a coin collection from a dedicated collector, coins acquired purely for financial reasons, or both to avoid spending your and the dealer's time.

Rare and precious coins are seldom found in coin bags, tubes, or boxes. More costly or unique coins are usually identified or distinguished from ordinary date coins in some way. All options are a coin book, individual cardboard coin containers, or certified coins from a reliable third-party grading organization.

Coins that have been professionally certified or graded are kept in sturdy acrylic containers and given a number and letter grade. It's important to read over the complete collection carefully to assess the sort of collection you have been assigned with and which outlet would be ideal to sell your collection.

It's critical to keep in mind that you shouldn't clean the coins. Cleaning a coin may permanently damage its surface and reduce its value, which is a typical error for non-collectors whenever they inherit coins. You'll always earn more money if you sell coins that have not been changed, regardless of the kind of coin (collectible, bullion, or numismatic).

How To Keep Your Coins Organized

Collect all of the loose quarters, dimes, dollars, mint or proof sets, and so on. This is usually done by coin type and denomination. Sort the coins and sets into comparable groups, such as the U.S. and international coins.

Consider putting bullion together as a group (silver, silver, palladium, and platinum coins, rounds, and bars). After dividing the coins by value, sort them further by kind for each denomination. For instance, split a group of silver dollars into distinct groupings such as Trade, Morgan, and Peace silver coins.

Those made of precious metals from other countries should be kept separate from coins made in the United States. Any paper cash may be identified and organized. Coins that are already in albums or cases should be kept alone since some of them may be limited mintage and key date coins, making it more straightforward for the coin dealer to recognize and price them separately.

You may use plastic tubes for vast quantities of coins of the same value, coin albums, or folders for arranging a run of sequential date coins to preserve the coins secure while you sort them.

Although 22 holders might assist in safeguarding the value of your most expensive coins, be cautious while employing mylar coin tosses. They may leave hairline dents on the coins' surface, lowering their value. To keep unusual or expensive coins secure, use separate coin holders or a storage box.

It's also critical that the coin spins you're using are composed of inert materials rather than PVC, which may degrade over time and stick to your coins.

Assess the Collection

Before contacting a coin dealer for a price, get a copy of a coin resource book to know how much each coin is valued or which coins are beautiful.

The Official "Blue Book," A Guidebook of United States Coins," is a well-known reference coin traders use to estimate wholesale price on most United States coins. The Blue Sheet from Coin Show Newsletter is another helpful resource.

These pricing recommendations are likely to make offerings at a decent reduction. Wikipedia might also help determine the mintage of several coins in the collection produced in the United States.

A word about price guides: they represent a moment in time of anticipated prices that might or might not correctly reflect your coins' current market and worth. While it is not a hard and fast rule, coins having mintages of million or less are usually considered collectible or numismatic.

Next, go over each set of coins and look for any unusual or possibly valuable coins using your pricing guides. After you've sorted the more expensive coins, get an estimate of the leftover expected date coins' count or an estimate of their weight in the event of an extensive collection.

To assess both the potential worth and the length of time it will take to examine your collection, a coin trader will have to know your collection's overall size and makeup.

When approaching coin dealers, it's good if you can give some information about your coin collection.

The coin trader will meticulously analyze your collection, list your coins & currencies, and value any unique, key date, or numismatic coins separately during the session.

If you believe a coin is extremely valuable or rare, you might consider getting it graded or verified by a specialist. The grade and mintage of a coin are by far the essential variables in

determining its worth, and most grading businesses will charge you depending on the coin's projected value.

It costs anywhere from $25 - $60 for each coin to have it graded, authenticated, and certified (and then put in a properly sealed plastic container). Handling shipping, insurance costs, and fees to and from the 3rdparty grading agency are not included. The added worth from the coin rating should be balanced against the costs and the possibility of greater interest from the party that buys your coins.

Please remember that most 3rd party grading services, including PCGS and NGC, demand a membership or subscription fee, which may be as much as $100. Furthermore, having your currency returned to you might take several weeks, adding time and price to your effort of selling the collection.

Selling Your Collection

There are several options for trading your coin collection. The ideal technique to market a collection depends on your situation and your time to finish the process. Court decrees or demands from the heirs may oblige you to sell the collection by a specific date, limiting your alternatives.

The following are the most typical and successful methods to sell coins:

- Selling your coins to a coin dealer
- Using an online auction to sell coins
- Making advantage of an auction house

Let's take a closer look at each choice

Coin Dealers

Your best alternative could be to trade your collection to a regional coin dealer or coin store if you want to sell it as fast as possible and at a reasonable price. Verify the coin dealer's BBB rating, professional certifications or associations, and internet ratings to ensure you are dealing with a trustworthy person or organization.

If you need numerous quotes from various dealers but do not have the resources and time to visit each one, try sending an itemized worksheet to coin dealers for a generic quotation. A Google Sheet or Excel document is the best option in most cases.

Many dealers will offer price information to know that changes may be necessary when the coins are physically inspected. To create a list like this, organize the coins, then input each coin's amount and overall state.

You do not need to include each coin for nickels, pennies, dimes, half dollars, quarters, or dollars unless it was a rare or essential date coin. For instance, all dimes struck before 1964 may be put together on the table without specifying each date separately.

In the same way, all quarters issued before 1965 may be classified together, and so on. List every coin by the producer or mint, kind, and denomination or size for silver, gold, palladium, and platinum coins.

Auction Houses

If you sell a significant collection of precious and rare coins, auction houses could be a suitable alternative. Usually, auction houses demand that the collection be worth at least $10,000.

Rather than offering the collection to a coin dealer, this approach may enable you to get somewhat better prices for individual pieces. However, bear in mind that your ultimate payment will be decreased after accounting for auction house commissions, fees (which are often in the 20percent range), and the time and price of shipping your collection to the auction site.

eBay

When trading a coin collection, auction platforms like eBay are one alternative. This helps you reach a wider audience, but taking individual images and uploading them online may be time-consuming.

Furthermore, costs for the listing, finale auction, and PayPal might cut the final sales price by 15percent or more. It would help if you also considered your responsibilities for packaging and delivering the products, as well as paying for sending and insurance, contacting bidders, and perhaps dealing with cancellations.

Whether you're selling or buying, consider that eBay may be a trap for exorbitant fees or dubious coins, so proceed with care.

Regardless of how you decide to sell your coin collection, try your best to learn as much as you can about the coins ahead of time, including recognizing low-mintmarks coins and evaluating prices. Arrange the coins by kind and year, do some research on trustworthy dealers and auction houses, and decide which is more essential to you: getting the best possible price for your coins (net of costs) or getting the process done quickly while still getting good values.

CONCLUSION

A decision to collect anything is one that is driven by enthusiasm. If you're passionate about something, whether it's something as simple as collecting pens or something as extravagant as collecting sports cars, you should be prepared to discuss it in-depth in case someone is interested in the items you've gathered. Additionally, it'd be a pointless exercise, effort, and resources if bogus objects contaminated your collection. Your long-established reputation will be ruined.

Numerous reasons exist for why individuals collect coins. Some collectors take pleasure in the historical aspects of their pastimes. Every coin is a true artifact from individuals who came many years, if not generations earlier. There were huge numbers of people holding these coins, several of whom you might well have heard of.

For a variety of reasons, people congregate many kinds of objects. Most of us have no desire whatsoever to assemble a salt & pepper sprinkle collection that fills an entire room. However, most of us find it incomprehensible why some people fail to appreciate the aesthetic value of Batman memorabilia. The goal of collecting anything is to pique curiosity and discover more about a subject you have a passion for. Although collecting is personal, everything has value to provide. The pursuit of coins is no different.

Coin collecting is done for a variety of purposes. Some people collect since they enjoy the historical aspect of the activity. Each coin represents a genuine piece of a person's daily life who lived many years or perhaps centuries ago. Huge numbers of people, several of whom you may have heard of, held such coins in their hands.

Others gather for financial gain or investment. Coin trading is a significant sector since coins are a market. Due to the hobby's rising popularity as well as the increased rarity that comes with age, coin collections improve in value over time. The possibility that perhaps a container of coins directly from the bank could, in a century or two, turn into a priceless treasure trove is one of the biggest draws, even for enthusiasts who have no interest in the business.

Since loose change may conceal certain surprises, the concept of collecting like a search for hidden riches is exactly what attracts many individuals to the activity for the first time. There are enough coins in use that are sufficiently old and scarce to be worth considerably far beyond their full price. Some individuals consider coin collecting to be dull. If so, they shouldn't pursue it as a hobby. Others, though, are enthralled by the mundane act of receiving change at the supermarket. The key towards becoming a competent coin collector would be to immerse yourself in the hobby by doing research on new discoveries as they are made. If there's a coin club in your neighborhood, consider joining it. You'll meet new people and discover numismatic information you didn't know existed.

Search the internet for groups that collect coins. You may find somebody who has the currency you're looking for and have a great opportunity to network as a result. You may have more opportunities to expand your collection and possibly earn some extra money from more and more coin collectors you know.

Thank you for taking the time to read this book. I wish you to start your collection as soon as possible!

71106856R00070